APPLIED MICROECONOMICS
Problems
in Estimation,
Forecasting,
and
Decision-making

APPLIED MICROECONOMICS

PROBLEMS
IN ESTIMATION,
FORECASTING,
AND
DECISION-MAKING

Richard Schmalensee

University of California
San Diego

 HOLDEN-DAY, INC.
San Francisco, Düsseldorf, Johannesburg, London
Panama, Singapore, Sydney, Toronto

Applied Microeconomics: Problems in Estimation, Forecasting,
    and Decision-making

Library of Congress Catalog Card Number: 72-83238
ISBN: 0-8162-7595-5

Printed in the United States of America

1234567890 MP 8079876543

To My Parents

PREFACE

This text describes a sequence of computer-based exercises in applied microeconomics; it is designed to supplement intermediate-level courses in microeconomic theory or managerial economics. In most economics courses today, especially those that follow the introductory sequence, the student's role is a passive one. The materials described here originated out of a belief that this is not as it should be: students seem to enjoy working on interesting problems, and they seem to learn most when challenged.

The tools and concepts needed for these exercises are generally presented herein, though the treatment of most topics is not intended to be complete. A working knowledge of elementary calculus is assumed, but the focus throughout is on understanding rather than rigor.

It is also assumed that a standard computer program for multiple regression analysis is available. All other programs employed by the instructor are discussed in the *Instructor's Manual.* These were coded mainly by Richard Butler, who also helped produce the *Manual*, and modified by Walter Maling. I would like to thank them both for their effort and ingenuity. All programs were written in FORTRAN IV; they have been tested on the IBM 360/65 at the Massachusetts Institute of Technology and the Burroughs B6700 at the University of California at San Diego.

The Sloan School of Management at MIT and the Edwin Land Foundation provided financial support for which I am most grateful. I am also greatly indebted to Paul MacAvoy for suggesting this project and for his continuing encouragement and advice as it progressed. Without him, these materials would not have been prepared.

I must thank all the students at MIT who suffered through several earlier versions of this material. They may have learned something; I certainly did.

The final version of this manuscript was skillfully and patiently typed by Marlene Moyes and Jane Nizyborski.

Last, by tradition, but certainly not least, I owe a great deal to my wife, Diane. She has cheerfully put up with more than her share of "working evenings" and "working weekends" as this effort has progressed. Further, her unceasing struggle to translate my writing into English is reflected in all that follows.

Richard Schmalensee

CONTENTS

INTRODUCTION

1

In economic theory courses, everything is known for certain. In the real world, nothing is. Applied work in economics seeks to understand some aspect of reality and then to use that understanding to aid decision-making. There is no definite right or wrong in such work; one does the best one can, avoids obvious errors, and lives with the results.

This text presents a sequence of problems which bear some relation to those encountered in the real world. While they should present a fair challenge, they are not intended to convey all of the difficulties encountered in actual applied work. (In particular, institutional considerations and measurement problems are not emphasized.) Rather, the focus here is on learning to use powerful tools and concepts in simple, but moderately challenging situations. These same approaches can be applied to more complex problems, though not as easily as they can be used here. The hope is that working on fairly simple problems which contain a dash of real-world ambiguity will make it easier for the student to deal with complicated situations of the same basic type—as well as providing an interesting way to learn some important tools.

The first three exercises involve analyzing historical data for a particular industry. In the industry to be analyzed, a large number of firms operated in the period for which data are provided. No technical change and no major shifts in consumers' tastes occurred in this period. Finally, each firm's output was either determined directly by the government or fixed by arbitrary nonprice rationing of an essential input factor. Because these conditions held, simple yet powerful statistical methods can be used to analyze the data, and Chapter 2 describes and discusses these methods.

Chapter 3 outlines the first two exercises and describes the history of the industry in more detail. From the data provided, students will be required to estimate the demand and cost relationships that characterize the industry to which they have been assigned. (The instructor will provide directions on the use of the particular statistical program to be employed.) Chapter 3 concludes with some suggestions about the two short reports students will write on these exercises.

Chapter 4 outlines the theory of price determination in competitive and monopolistic markets and discusses the simple mathematics on which it is based. Students will apply this theory to their industry. For given values of certain variables, they will forecast the price and output of their industry under conditions of competition and of monopoly. This exercise is discussed in Chapter 5.

The next chapter (Chapter 6) examines price determination in oligopolistic markets, markets with few firms. Under these circumstances, firms' expectations about their competitors' behavior become an important determinant of industry performance. This so complicates the firms' decisions that no truly general theories of oligopolistic pricing have yet been developed.

To provide a deeper understanding of the problem of pricing in concentrated markets than can be obtained by passively reading about it, the last exercise involves making pricing decisions under conditions of oligopoly. Chapter 7 describes a simulation exercise in which each student will be on the board of directors of a firm with few competitors. Each firm's profits depend on the prices of all other firms in the same market, and individuals will attempt to maximize the profits of their firms. At the end of the exercise, the behavior and performance of the firms and industries simulated will be analyzed in terms of their structure and the theoretical notions outlined in Chapter 6.

All four of these exercises are related. The statistical estimations should provide some idea of the cost function of a typical one-plant firm and the demand curve faced by that firm when all producers charge the same price. In the forecasting problem, students will be given the number of firms operating in the industry during the period for which data were provided. This makes possible construction of an estimate of the industry's demand function and of a forecast of short-run and long-run competitive and monopoly prices. This estimate of the short-run monopoly price will be extremely useful in the decision-making exercise, since if all firms in an industry charge this price they will maximize total industry profits. In this exercise the demand function originally estimated will be the curve facing each firm if they all charge the same price. When prices differ within an industry, however, students will have to learn by experience the impact of price differentials on firms' demands.

Finally, none of the four exercises will necessarily be the same from class to class. The instructor can provide data corresponding to a large number of different cost and demand functions, and the market structures encountered in the decision-making exercise can vary considerably from industry to industry.

Most of the discussions in this book are self-contained, so that no other works are cited in the text. References are provided at the ends of Chapters 2 to 4 and 6, however, for those who wish to read more on the topics covered there.

ECONOMETRIC METHODS

2

What is Econometrics?

Economics attempts to be a science, and therefore economists are interested in explaining and predicting certain phenomena. Economic theory enables us to make some predictions, but these normally relate only to directions of change. We expect, for instance, that if a monopolist lowers his price his sales will increase. Sometimes even this vague sort of prediction is denied us; no pure theory exists which tells us whether the gross national product (GNP) will rise or fall next year.

Economic theory does, however, point to the existence of certain fairly stable relationships involving relevant economic variables. These can often be expressed as equations. To make predictions and decisions we need to know what those equations actually look like; we need real-world numbers. This need gave rise to econometrics, which is often defined as the *measurement of relationships suggested by economic theory.* Econometrics also employs a set of techniques for testing propositions suggested by economic theory, as we will see below.

Economic theory emphasizes the interdependence of economic systems. Any one quantity, such as the price of ice cream, is influenced by a virtually infinite number of other quantities. If we wish to construct a useable demand curve for ice cream, though, we simply can't consider all possible variables. We must make a judgment about which are important. We might, for instance, decide that the main variables influencing the demand for ice cream are the weather, the price of ice cream, the general level of other prices, consumers' incomes, the age distribution of the population, and advertising of ice cream.

We would then group all other influences into an *error or disturbance term.* In addition to containing the impact of variables we could measure but choose not to (such as the price of hot dogs), it reflects quantities which vary irregularly but which are virtually impossible to quantify (such as consumer tastes) and errors in measuring the variables we have chosen to consider explicitly. We treat the disturbance term as a *random variable,* a chance-determined quantity whose values cannot be perfectly forecast. From the way we define it, the disturbance term cannot be observed.

Formally, then, we begin econometric work by developing equations of the following form:

$$V = f(Z_1, \ldots, Z_m, e) \qquad (2\text{-}1)$$

The *dependent variable* is V, and the N quantities Z_1, $Z_2, \ldots, Z_m$ are the principal *independent variables* influencing V. Other forces are summarized in the disturbance term, *e*. This equation is assumed to hold for all observations of V and the Z's. (An observation may be the values taken on by the variables in a particular year or other time period, or the data may be composed of observations relating to individual states or households or other units in a single time period. These two types of observations are termed *time series* and *cross section*, respectively.) Given observations on the Z's and V, one task of econometrics is to describe the function $f(\cdot)$ as well as possible. Another task is to test for the presence of certain properties of this function. [If (2-1) represents the demand curve for ice cream, for instance, with V the quantity demanded and Z_1 the advertising of ice cream, we might want to test whether or not $\partial f/\partial Z_1$ is greater than zero.]

Economic theory may suggest something about the function $f(\cdot)$. Often it predicts the signs of the partial derivatives. For instance, we expect the quantity of ice cream demanded to decline as the price of ice cream rises. Sometimes other information is available as well. Consumer demand theory says that if all prices and incomes double, a consumer's purchases should remain unchanged. Textbook theory is not the only source of knowledge, of course; common sense is useful too. We expect ice cream sales to vary directly with temperature in most situations.

All information provided by theory and other sources should be incorporated into econometric analysis, though rarely does such a priori information completely determine the form of the unknown function $f(\cdot)$. Economic theory and introspection are best thought of as sources of *hypotheses* about $f(\cdot)$, hypotheses which must be tested before being accepted.

For computational simplicity, we work, whenever it is sensible to do so, with functions that are linear in a finite number of unknown parameters. That is, we deal with special cases of (2-1) of the form

$$Y(V) = b_1 X_1 (Z_1, Z_2, \ldots, Z_m)$$
$$+ b_2 X_2 (Z_1, Z_2, \ldots, Z_m) + \cdots$$
$$+ b_n X_n (Z_1, Z_2, \ldots, Z_m) + e \qquad (2\text{-}2)$$

The b's are the unknown parameters we wish to estimate. The functions $Y(\cdot)$ and $X_1(\cdot), X_2(\cdot), \ldots, X_n(\cdot)$ are specified by the investigator.

Special cases of (2-2) are, for instance, the following:

$$V = b_1 Z_1 + b_2 Z_2 + e$$

$$\log (V) = b_1 \log (Z_1) + b_2 \log (Z_2) + e$$

$$V = b_1 + b_2 Z_1 + b_3 (Z_1)^2 + e$$

In the third of these examples, b_1 is multiplied by a variable which is always equal to one, giving the model an *intercept* or *constant term*.

Only rarely does economic theory greatly restrict the choice of functions in (2-2). In general, these functions should be chosen so as to be moderately simple and easy to work with. The information in the data can then be used to select the best functional forms, where the usual criterion involves the ability of the estimated relation to predict changes in V, the dependent variable.

The most common technique employed to estimate the b's in an equation of the form of (2-2) is called *ordinary least-squares regression* or *multiple linear regression*. The mechanics involved in this procedure are easily outlined. Suppose we have some set of estimates of the b's in (2-2)—call these $\hat{b}_1$, $\hat{b}_2, \ldots, \hat{b}_n$. Also suppose we have T observations on Y and on $X_1, X_2, \ldots, X_n$. Let $Y(t)$ be the tth observation on Y, $X_1(t)$ the tth observation on X_1, and so on. We then write the definitions

$$\hat{e}(t) = Y(t) - \hat{b}_1 X_1(t) - \hat{b}_2 X_2(t) - \cdots - \hat{b}_n X_n(t)$$
$$\text{for } t = 1, 2, \ldots, T \quad (2\text{-}3)$$

This equation defines the estimated error, $\hat{e}(t)$, often called the *residual,* for each observation for the given estimates of the b's.

Least-squares estimation consists of choosing the $\hat{b}$'s so as to minimize the sum of squared residuals, $\sum_{t=1}^{T} \hat{e}(t)^2$. A rule such as this for obtaining estimates of unknown parameters is called an *estimator.*

The main purpose of this chapter is to provide an elementary understanding of the properties of this estimator and of the interpretation of the estimates it produces.

First, however, we must consider situations in which the use of least squares is not appropriate. Least squares is unsuitable when the model considered involves variables which are mutually determined, through a system of simultaneous equations. Such situations are discussed in the next section. We then turn to some essential statistical notions.

The last two sections of this chapter then discuss linear regression, first in statistical terms and then from the viewpoint of a user who wishes to interpret computer output from a regression program.

Simultaneous Equations

Consider a simple linear supply-demand system where price, P, and quality, Q, are determined by the following pair of simultaneous equations:

$$P = b_1 + b_2 Q + e \qquad \text{supply curve}$$
$$Q = b_3 - b_4 P + u \qquad \text{demand curve} \tag{2-4}$$

Here e and u are disturbance terms, and the b_i are constants. Suppose you were given data on this market for a long period of time. Could you estimate the supply and demand curves? The answer is clearly no, since all the observations on P and Q would be clustered around the equilibrium point $[P = (b_1 + b_2 b_3) / (1 + b_2 b_4), Q = (b_3 - b_1 b_4) / (1 + b_2 b_4)]$, and you have no way of relating the shape of the cluster to the parameters of either curve. If you knew that u was always zero, your task would be simpler. Then shifts in e would move the supply curve, and all the observations would lie along the demand curve. Estimation of b_3 and b_4 would pose no problems, but there would be no way to use the data to estimate the parameters of the supply curve. If you knew that u varied much less from observation to observation than e, the same sort of argument would apply. The supply curve would then have moved much more than the demand curve. Most of the data would lie near the demand curve, and you could get some idea of its shape.

In a classic early study of the demand for agricultural commodities, this notion was employed. The argument was that supply varied a great deal depending on the weather, but that little random movement in the demand curve was to be expected. In this situation, we say that the demand curve is *identified,* that is, it is potentially capable of being estimated from the data, while the supply curve is not identified (or under-identified).

Suppose now that u and e in (2-4) show about the same variation from observation to observation, but that demand depends on the level of income as well as price. Then changes in income will move the demand curve and thus trace out the supply curve. The supply curve is identified because of the variable *exogenous* to (determined outside of) the system of equations we are dealing with. If supply also depends on rainfall, and if rainfall can be measured, it can be shown that both curves are identified.

Most econometrics texts discuss the identification

problem in considerable detail, but the basic notion is that presented here. In order for a particular equation in a system of simultaneous equations to be identified, something must be present in the system which shifts the other equations but leaves the equation under consideration unaltered and thus tends to trace it out.

Suppose that (2-4) is expanded to the following system:

$$P = b_1 + b_2 Q + b_5 R + e \qquad \text{supply curve}$$
$$Q = b_3 - b_4 P + b_6 Y + u \qquad \text{demand curve}$$

(2-5)

Here b_5 and b_6 are constants, R is rainfall, and Y is consumer income. As mentioned just above, Eqs. (2-5) are identified. Can we use simple linear regression to estimate the six unknown constants? The answer is generally no.

As written above, (2-5) is composed of *structural equations,* equations suggested by the theory. If you solve (2-5) for P and Q, you obtain two *reduced-form equations* in which the endogenous variables P and Q are functions of the exogenous variables R and Y and of the disturbance terms e and u. Since both P and Q depend on both e and u, it is clear that e and Q will move together in the supply equation. If e and Q are correlated in this fashion, least squares will give results that are biased and inconsistent in the statistician's terminology and generally misleading.

The basic character of the problem is simple. Suppose e is large whenever Q is. We cannot observe e, though. Thus the effects of both e and Q on P will be attributed to Q, and any method of estimating b_2 that does not take this into account is likely to come up with an estimate above the true value of this parameter.

Figure 2.1 illustrates this discussion. We assume that data are generated according to the equation

$$Y = b_0 + b_1 X + e$$

where e is, as usual, a disturbance term. This equation, with $e = 0$, is shown as line TT in the figure. Assume that e is positively related to X: whenever e is large, X will tend to be large also. In this case, the data will be as shown in the figure, where each "o" represents an observation of X and Y. Looking only at the data, one would take the line EE as a good estimate of the (unknown) true line. But such an estimate, which would be yielded by least squares, would clearly be misleading. Formally, the estimated

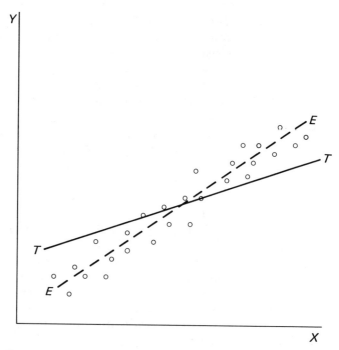

Figure 2.1   Illustration of biased estimates.

parameters are *biased* and *inconsistent*; no matter how many observations we obtained, our estimates would still differ systematically from the true values of b_0 and b_1.

Two problems are thus associated with models involving systems of simultaneous equations. The first is *identification*: one must determine whether it is theoretically possible to "sort out" the coefficients of the structural equations from observable data generated by the true system. This issue must be considered even when there are no error terms present in the system, as the discussion below Eqs. (2-4) should indicate. The second problem is that of *estimation*: given that least squares is an inappropriate estimator, alternatives must be found.

Basic Statistical Concepts

Before we can discuss least-squares regression, we must venture into the realm of general statistical analysis. We have said that we treat the disturbance or error term in an econometric equation as a *random variable,* a chance-determined quantity. By definition, the particular values of a random variable one will observe cannot ever be precisely predicted. Certain properties of random variables must be understood in order to make use of least squares—or, for that matter, any estimator.

Suppose we have a black box with a crank. Every time the crank is turned a lot of noise is made and a poker chip is ejected. On each poker chip is a real number, not necessarily an integer. Suppose the box prints numbers on the chips in such a way that it is theoretically impossible to predict the precise sequence of numbers that will be observed. It then makes sense to treat each observed number as an observation of a random variable; we shall call this random variable x.

Suppose we take the box apart. By assumption, this will still not enable us to predict individual values of x. If we really understand the mechanism, though, we should be able to give the probability that the next number observed will be less than or equal to a, for any real number a. We can summarize this knowledge, which is really all that can be known about a random variable, in the *distribution function* $F_x(x)$, defined so that $F_x(a)$ is the probability that x will be less than or equal to a for any real number a. It is clear that for $b > a$, Prob $(a < x < b)$, the probability that x is greater than a but less than or equal to b is equal to $F_x(b) - F_x(a)$.

When x is not limited to a finite number of possible values, the derivative of $F_x(x)$ exists in all cases of interest to us. We define

$$f_x(x) = (d/dx)[F_x(x)]$$

and call $f_x(x)$ the *density function* of x. The fundamental theorem of calculus then yields

$$\text{Prob } (a < x \leq b) = F_x(b) - F_x(a) = \int_a^b f_x(t)\, dt \quad (2\text{-}6)$$

In words, the probability that a particular value of x will lie between a and b is the area under the density function between a and b. The density function must always be nonnegative to make any sense, since probabilities cannot be less than zero. Also, the integral of $f_x(x)$ from $-\infty$ to $+\infty$ must equal one, since some number is on each poker chip.

A simple example may help to clarify these concepts. Suppose that upon examining the innards of our black box we deduce that the number printed will always be between zero and one. Further, we find that the probability that x will be less than or equal to $1/2$ is $1/2$, less than or equal to $1/4$ is $1/4$, and, in general, the probability that x will be less than or equal to k is equal to k, for any k between zero and one. We can then write down the distribution function of this variable as

$$F_x(x) = \begin{cases} 0 & \text{for } x \leq 0 \\ x & \text{for } 0 < x \leq 1 \\ 1 & \text{for } x > 1 \end{cases}$$

Differentiating, we obtain the corresponding density function

$$f_x(x) = \begin{cases} 0 & \text{for } x \leq 0 \\ 1 & \text{for } 0 < x \leq 1 \\ 0 & \text{for } x > 1 \end{cases}$$

A random variable with this density function is said to be uniformly distributed between zero and one.

Remember that we know the density function only because we have dismantled the black box. In the real world, we never know for sure the exact form of any density function we are interested in. [Of course, if we have a number of observations on x, the fraction falling between a and b is an estimate of the integral in (2-6). Intuitively, if we have a lot of observations and consider a lot of intervals, we will have a pretty good idea of the shape of the unknown density. But we can never be *certain* that we have not observed an atypical set of x's.]

The density (or distribution) function of a random variable contains all the information that is knowable about its behavior. Sometimes we need to know less, however, and we can often summarize the relevant information by computing various *expected values* or *expectations*. The expected value of any function $g(x)$ of the random variable x is written as $E[g(\mathrm{x})]$ and is defined by

$$E[g(x)] = \int_{-\infty}^{+\infty} g(x) f_x(x) \, dx \qquad (2\text{-}7)$$

The expected value of $g(x)$ is a weighted average of the values of $g(x)$, where the weights are the probabilities of their occurrence.

Suppose, for instance, that $f_x(x)$ is positive for all positive x and that $g(x)$ is equal to one for x less than or equal to five and 10 for x greater than five. We can then compute $E[g(x)]$ as follows:

$$E[g(x)] = \int_{-\infty}^{5} 1 f_x(x)\, dx + \int_{5}^{+\infty} 10 f_x(x)\, dx$$

$$= 1 \int_{-\infty}^{5} f_x(x)\, dx + 10 \left[1 - \int_{-\infty}^{5} f_x(x)\, dx \right]$$

$$= 10 - 9 F_x(5)$$

The first step follows because the integral of a density function from minus infinity to plus infinity must equal one, and the second step employs the definition relating the density and distribution functions.

Two common and useful expected values are the following:

$$E[x] = \mu_x = \text{the mean of } x$$

$$E[(x - \mu_x)^2] = \sigma_x^2 = \text{the variance of } x$$

The *mean* of x is a measure of the central tendency of the distribution, an indication of the average value of x. The *variance,* on the other hand, measures the spread or dispersion of x around its mean. The positive square root of the variance, written σ_x, is called the *standard deviation* of x.

These quantities can be calculated quite easily for the uniform distribution presented above:

$$\mu_x = E(x) = \int_{-\infty}^{+\infty} x f_x(x)\, dx = \int_{0}^{1} x(1)\, dx$$

$$= (x^2/2) \Big|_{0}^{1} = 1/2$$

$$\sigma_x^2 = E[(x - \mu_x)^2] = \int_{-\infty}^{+\infty}[x - 1/2]^2 f_x(x)\, dx$$

$$= \int_0^1 [x - 1/2]^2 (1)\, dx = \int_0^1 [x^2 - x + 1/4]\, dx$$

$$= [(x^3/3) - (x^2/2) + (x/4)] \Big|_0^1 = 1/12$$

$$\sigma_x = \sqrt{1/12} = 1/2\sqrt{3}$$

We need two further definitions. Imagine another black box that produces poker chips with two numbers on them, one labeled x and the other labeled y. Reasoning as above, dismantling the box would give us enough information to write down the *joint density function* of the two random variables. This function is defined by

Prob $(a < x \le b$ and $c < y \le d)$

$$= \int_a^b \int_c^d f_{xy}(x,y)\, dy\, dx \quad (2\text{-}8)$$

The natural generalization of definition (2-7) enables us to talk of the expected value of any function $g(x,y)$ of x and y.

$$E[g(x,y)] = \int_{-\infty}^{+\infty} \int_{-\infty}^{+\infty} g(x,y) f_{xy}(x,y)\, dx\, dy$$

Two of these expected values are of great interest to us. The definitions are

$$E[(x - \mu_x)(y - \mu_y)] = \text{cov }(x,y)$$
$$= \text{the covariance of } x \text{ and } y$$

$$\text{cov }(x,y)/\sigma_x \sigma_y = \rho(x,y)$$
$$= \text{the correlation coefficient of } x \text{ and } y$$

The *covariance* is a measure of association. If both variables are always above and below their means at the same time, the covariance will be positive. If x is above its mean when y is below its mean and vice versa, the covariance will be negative. The covariance may have any value, depending on the size of x and y. If x were measured in inches instead of feet, for instance, the covariance of x with any other random variable would be multiplied by 12.

The *correlation coefficient* is a measure of association that does not suffer from this defect. The correlation coefficient will always be between -1 and $+1$. It takes on these values if $y = a + bx$, with a and b constants, where $b < 0$ implies $\rho = -1$ and $b > 0$ implies $\rho = +1$.

Suppose we have a *sample* of T observations on a random variable x; call these observations x_1, $x_2, \ldots, x_T$. How can we use them to learn about the unknown density function from which they came? One approach was described parenthetically below Eq. (2-6), but it is rarely used unless T is very large. Another line of attack involves estimating the moments of the density function. Recall that the true moments involved averaging over the true density function, thus weighting by the true or *population* probabilities. We can estimate moments by averaging over the observed or *sample* probabilities. We could estimate the true or population mean of x, μ_x, for instance, by the *sample mean:*

$$\hat{\mu}_x = (1/T) \sum_{i=1}^{T} x_i$$

[Throughout this chapter, a hat $(\hat{\ })$ denotes a function of sample values.] The population variance of x could be similarly estimated from our data by the *sample variance:*

$$\hat{\sigma}_x^2 = (1/T) \sum_{i=1}^{T} (x_i - \hat{\mu}_x)^2$$

Since the x_i are random variables, because they will differ in an unpredictable way from one sample of size T to another, so are $\hat{\mu}_x$ and $\hat{\sigma}_x^2$. This notion should not be too difficult. Suppose one throws a single die 10 times, counts the number of times it comes up six, and divides this number by 10. This procedure provides an estimator of the probability that the die will come up six on any toss. It is a random variable, though, since the estimate or number it yields will generally vary from one set of tosses to another in an unpredictable way.

This may begin to sound relevant to econometrics. In working with a model of the form of (2-2), we assume that there are true, underlying population values of the b's that generated the data we have collected. We want to obtain a set of estimates of them for use in decision-making. These estimates will depend on the exact values taken on by the (unobservable) disturbance term in the particular sample we have. Since our estimators of the b's will generally depend on Y and thus on the random variable e, they are also random variables. In order to evaluate some set of estimates, for instance, to decide how precise they are, we need to assume something about the density function of the error term.

The most common assumption and the most useful one is that the error term in (2-2) is *normally distributed*. The density function of a normally distributed random variable x is given by

$$f_x(x) = (1/\sigma_x\sqrt{2\pi}) \exp\left[\frac{-(x - \mu_x)^2}{2\sigma_x{}^2}\right] \quad -\infty \leq x \leq +\infty$$

Notice that this function depends only on two parameters: its mean μ_x and its standard deviation σ_x. If a random variable is thought to be normally distributed, an estimate of its density function can be written as soon as estimates of the mean and variance are calculated.

Figure 2.2 shows graphs of the normal density function for various values of the parameters. It

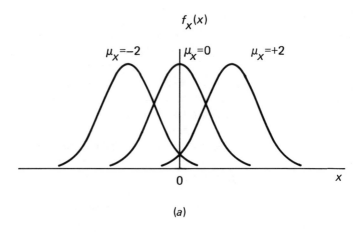

(a)

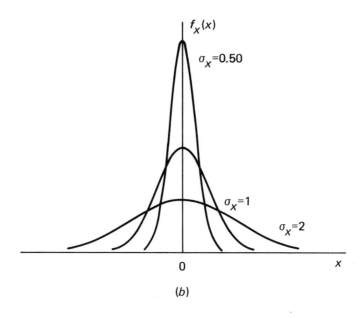

(b)

Figure 2.2 Comparison of different normal density functions:
(a) different means, $\sigma_x = 1$; (b) different variances, $\mu_x = 0$.

should be clear that the mean indicates central tendency, while the variance measures dispersion.

The most common rationale for using the normal distribution in econometrics is based on the Central Limit theorem. This theorem says, roughly, that the distribution of the sum of a very large number of random variables, each with a very small variance, approaches the normal distribution as the number of variables becomes very large and the variance of each becomes very small. Though the theorem strictly describes only what happens in the limit, the approximation is quite good for moderate numbers of variables. (Consider the sample mean, $\hat{\mu}_x$, as defined above, as the sum of x_i/T, $i = 1, 2, \ldots, T$. As T becomes very large, the distribution of $\hat{\mu}_x$ approaches the normal. For most densities, this distribution can be approximated quite accurately by the normal for T above 20.) This relates to our earlier discussion of the error or disturbance term as the net result of a large number of small forces, so the assumption of a normal distribution is quite natural. Least squares is a good estimator even if this assumption is wrong, and the testing procedures we discuss below are fairly reliable if the assumption is even approximately correct.

Two useful properties of normally distributed variables (which can be verified from standard tables) are the basis for the tests we will be concerned with in our discussion of least squares:

$$\text{Prob } [|x - \mu_x| \geq 1.96\sigma_x] = .05$$

$$\text{Prob } [|x - \mu_x| \geq 2.58\sigma_x] = .01$$

In words, the probability that a single observation of a normally distributed random variable x will be 1.96 or more standard deviations away from its mean is .05. The probability that it will be 2.58 or more standard deviations away is .01.

Suppose we know the variance of a normally distributed random variable, but we do not know its mean. We have T independent observations on the variable, and we compute the sample mean, $\hat{\mu}_x$, defined above. What does this estimate tell us about the true mean? It is easy to show that if a random variable x, not necessarily normally distributed, has a standard deviation σ_x, the estimator $\hat{\mu}_x$, which is also a random variable, has standard deviation $\sigma_x/\sqrt{T}$. If x is normally distributed with mean μ_x, $\hat{\mu}_x$ is also normally distributed with mean μ_x.

Suppose that we have $T=25$ independent observations on a particular variable x with known standard deviation equal to five. Thus the quantity $\hat{\mu}_x$ is normally distributed with standard deviation one $(=5/\sqrt{25})$. Suppose the sample mean is equal to five. If the population mean were 1.9, the probability that we would observe a sample mean of five is less than .01, since five is more than 2.58 standard deviations away from 1.9. Now the population mean is a fixed, though unknown, number, and we can't really say that it is unlikely to be equal to 1.9. It either is 1.9 or it isn't. What we can say is that *it is very unlikely that we would have obtained the observations we actually got if the population mean were outside the interval 2.42−7.58. This is a key notion, and it underlies the theories* of *hypothesis testing* and *confidence intervals.*

We have just seen an example of the latter. We expressed confidence in the above example that the true population mean lay in the interval 2.42−7.58. Since the probability is .99 that the sample mean, $\hat{\mu}_x$, falls in the interval $\mu_x - 2.58$ to $\mu_x + 2.58$, the probability is also .99 that the interval $\hat{\mu}_x - 2.58$ to $\hat{\mu}_x + 2.58$ contains μ_x. In general, we say that a 99% confidence interval on the mean of a normal distribution with known variance is given by

$$\hat{\mu}_x - 2.58\sigma_x/\sqrt{T} < \mu_x < \hat{\mu}_x + 2.58\sigma_x/\sqrt{T} \qquad (2\text{-}9)$$

where the sample mean, $\hat{\mu}_x$, is based on T observations. Similarly, in the example above a 95% confidence interval is $\hat{\mu}_x - 1.96$ to $\hat{\mu}_x + 1.96$, and the general interval is

$$\hat{\mu}_x - 1.96\sigma_x/\sqrt{T} < \mu_x < \hat{\mu}_x + 1.96\sigma_x/\sqrt{T} \qquad (2\text{-}10)$$

Procedures for constructing confidence intervals on unknown parameters are closely related to the methods used to test hypotheses about those parameters. Still considering the example above, suppose we have a special interest in whether or not the mean is equal to one. We then choose as our *null hypothesis,* the hypothesis to be tested, the assertion $\mu_x = 1$. We saw above that 1.0 lies outside the 99% confidence interval on the mean. Hence it is unlikely that we would observe what we did in fact observe if the mean were one. This, intuitively, suggests rejection of the null hypothesis.

More formally, consider the general null hypothesis $\mu_x = Q$. Suppose we decide to reject this hypothesis whenever Q falls outside the interval defined by (2-9). If the null hypothesis is true, the probability of rejecting it with this method is .01, the probability that the (random) interval defined by (2-9) does not include the true mean. If we decided instead to reject the hypothesis whenever Q lay outside the shorter interval defined by (2-10), the probability of rejecting it if it is true would be .05. Of course, because the interval is shorter, the probability of accepting the null hypothesis when $\mu_x \neq Q$ would be lower.

Considering (2-9), (2-10), and the above discussion, it should be clear that when x is normally distributed with known standard deviation, the following statistic provides a test of the null hypothesis $\mu_x = Q$:

$$\tau = (\hat{\mu}_x - Q)/(\sigma_x/\sqrt{T}) \qquad (2\text{-}11)$$

If this statistic is greater than 1.96 in absolute value, the null hypothesis is said to be rejected at the 5% significance level. If τ is greater than 2.58 in absolute value, the null hypothesis is rejected at the 1% significance level. In general, the significance level of a test is 100 times the probability of rejecting the null hypothesis if it is true.

In any statistical analysis, one's null hypothesis should be chosen so as to have a sensible interpretation. In a study of the effect of fertilizer on crop yields, one logical null hypothesis is that there is no effect; this is certainly of interest to a potential user of the fertilizer. In demand analysis, a sensible null hypothesis might be that the price elasticity of demand equals −1. Rejection of this hypothesis would then imply elastic or inelastic demand.

A very common null hypothesis in connection with models of the form of (2-2) is that one of the true b's is zero. If b_j is zero, this means that, given the assumed functions, X_j does not affect Y. The quantity X_j then does not belong in the equation. The hypothesis that b_j equals zero is a natural one to test, then, if we are not absolutely certain that X_j influences Y. If this null hypothesis is rejected at the 5% level, we say that the coefficient b_j is significantly different from zero (or *significant*) at the 5% level. In some sense, rejection of $b_j = 0$ means that X_j probably does matter and should be left in the equation. If the null hypothesis cannot be rejected, the variable is often dropped and the equation reestimated without it. The general rationale is that the fewer the coefficients being estimated from a given number of observations, the more reliable will be the estimate of each coefficient.

How do we test the hypothesis $b_j = 0$? We mentioned above that the least-squares estimators of the b's are random variables, since they depend on the (unobservable) values taken on by the disturbance term. If the disturbance term is normally distributed, it can be shown that the $\hat{b}$'s are also. The true means of these random variables are, as it turns out, the true b's—provided some assumptions discussed below are valid. The standard deviations of these estimators, however, are not known a priori. It is possible to estimate them, though, and all standard regression programs do this.

We outlined above a test of hypotheses about the true mean, μ_x, of a normal population, which made use of an estimator $\hat{\mu}_x$ which was normally distributed with mean μ_x and known standard deviation $\sigma_x/\sqrt{T}$. In linear regression, we have estimators $\hat{b}_i$ with means b_i and estimated standard deviations $\hat{\sigma}_i$. It seems logical, and is in fact correct, that some modification of the test presented above could be used to test hypotheses about the b_i. We discuss the necessary modification in the latter part of the next section. First, though, we shall examine the assumptions underlying multiple linear regression and its properties.

Regression: Assumptions and Properties

For convenience, let us rewrite the basic model (2-2) in the following form:

$$Y(t) = b_1 X_1(t) + \cdots + b_n X_n(t) + e(t) \qquad (2\text{-}12)$$

The variables Y and $X_1, X_2, \ldots, X_n$ may be functions of more basic quantities, such as V and $Z_1, Z_2, \ldots, Z_m$ in (2-2). Writing (2-2) as (2-12) amounts to defining new variables; it costs us no generality and simplifies the notation. We assume there are T observations on all variables in (2-12), so that t runs from 1 to T.

We have already described in a general way how least-squares estimates are calculated, and for our purposes a more detailed examination of the mechanics involved would add nothing. The question now before us is whether the least-squares estimator is a good one or not. The answer to this depends both on the assumptions we make about the situation being modeled and on how one defines "good," since there are a number of properties that are desirable in an estimation method. We now consider some of the more commonly discussed desirable properties and indicate when ordinary least squares possesses them.

First, an estimation method should be moderately simple, in the sense that the required computations are not unduly burdensome. Least squares has this property, since it is a *linear estimator*; it can be shown that the $\hat{b}$'s are linear functions of the observations on Y. This suggests, correctly, that linear regression is about as simple a method as one could hope to find.

A second desirable property is that the estimates not differ systematically from the true values. One measure of this property is called bias. An estimator of b's in Eq. (2-11) is said to be *unbiased* if $E[\hat{b}_i] = b_i$ for all i. Least-squares estimators will be unbiased, in general, if the following assumptions hold:

1. $E[e(t)] = 0$, all t. The error term has a mean of zero.
2. cov $[X_i(t+\tau), e(t)] = 0$, all i, t, and τ. The error term is independent of the independent variables.
3. It is never the case that $c_1 X_1(t) + \cdots + c_n X_n(t)$ equals zero for all t unless all the c's equal zero. No set of independent variables move exactly together.

In many situations, one of the X_i, say X_1, is equal to one for all t, so that the equation has an intercept term. If this is true then it is easy to show that Assumption 3 implies that it is not the case for any i

and j not equal to one or to each other that $X_i(t) = a + bX_j(t)$ for all t with a and b nonzero. (If this equation holds, $c_1X_1 + c_iX_i + c_jX_j$ is always zero if $c_1 = -c_ia$ and $c_j = -c_ib$.) Recalling our discussion of the correlation coefficient above, this means that no two independent variables can be perfectly correlated if the regression has an intercept. That is, the correlation coefficient between them cannot equal -1 or $+1$.

In time-series analysis, it is often the case that one of the X's in (2-11) is equal to the value that Y assumed in an earlier period. Such quantities are referred to as *lagged dependent variables*. When an equation contains one or more lagged dependent variables, the following assumption must be added to Assumptions 1–3 in order to ensure that the estimates will be unbiased for large samples:

4. cov $[e(t), e(t + \tau)] = 0$, all t and τ. The errors corresponding to different observations are independent.

(Whenever lagged dependent variables are present in a regression the $\hat{b}_i$ will be biased in small samples. This bias is usually neglected in practice as long as Assumption 4 holds.)

A third property that a good estimator should have is *efficiency*. We would like the estimated values to be as close as possible to the true values. It can be shown that if we add one more assumption to Assumptions 1–4, the least-squares estimator will be efficient in the sense that $E[(\hat{b}_i - b_i)^2]$ will be lower for all i than for the $\hat{b}_i$ generated by any other linear, unbiased estimator. That assumption is

5. $E[e(t)^2] = \sigma_e^2$, a constant for all t. The variance of the error term is the same for all observations.

One last assumption is often made when linear regression is used:

6. $e(t)$ is normally distributed for all t.

As mentioned above, this assumption ensures that the $\hat{b}_i$ will be normally distributed.

We now discuss what happens to least squares when Assumptions 1–5 fail. Assumption 1, that the error term have zero mean, is not an issue if the regression equation contains a constant term. It will then be impossible to tell whether the estimate of the constant corresponds to the true value of the constant term or to a nonzero mean value of the errors. But it is difficult to imagine a situation in which this distinction would matter. A very important fact of least squares is that when there is a constant term (intercept) present in the estimated equation, the computed residuals [as defined by Eq. (2-3)] sum to zero identically.

Assumption 2, the assumption that the disturbance is independent of the independent variables, is violated in simultaneous-equations models, as we discussed earlier. Also, this assumption is violated when lagged dependent variables are used as independent variables. In either case, biased estimates will be obtained from least squares. In the simultaneous-equations case, alternative estimators are usually employed. This assumption cannot be tested using the data, since it is a property of least squares that the residuals will have zero sample covariance with each of the independent variables in the equation.

If Assumption 3 as stated above is violated, so that a linear equation involving the independent variables is always satisfied, it is literally impossible to compute least-squares estimates. (The computer will try to divide by zero—and fail.) This is not a common problem; what often happens, though, is that an equation such as the one in Assumption 3 holds almost exactly. This problem is called *multicolline-*

arity. When two variables, say, X_1 and X_2, are very closely correlated, it is hard for you or the computer to tell which changes in Y are due to changes in X_1 and which are caused by changes in X_2. If the two variables are expected to move together in the future, there is no problem in terms of forecasting; one variable is simply dropped from the equation, and when the regression is reestimated the other picks up the effects of both on Y. If you are interested in the separate impact of the correlated variables, though, the problem is more difficult. Occasionally, the theory underlying the equation may suggest a solution. The usual textbook answer is "get more data," but this may not be possible. Nature does not always perform the experiments we would like her to.

There is no hard and fast way to tell if multicollinearity is causing trouble. If all the coefficients are significant, there is usually nothing to worry about. If several coefficients are not significant, and dropping one or more variables makes some of these significant, multicollinearity is usually causing trouble. A glance at the correlation coefficients of pairs of independent variables (if available) may indicate the source of the problem.

The assumption that disturbance terms are independent, Assumption 4, is mainly an issue in time-series studies. When the error terms from different (usually adjacent) time periods are correlated, the problem is described as *autocorrelation* or *serial correlation* of the errors. When Assumption 4 is violated, least-squares estimates are not efficient, and they are biased, even in large samples (even as T increases without bound), if lagged dependent variables are present. There are tests, involving the computed residuals, for simple sorts of autocorrelation, and corrections can be made to produce unbiased, efficient estimators. We examine the most common test for autocorrelation in the last section of this chapter.

Besides indicating that the error-generating mechanism is not what we would prefer, the presence of autocorrelation in the residuals may signal another problem which is usually the source of the observed serial correlation. Systematic movement of the estimated errors often arises through *misspecification.* There are two types of misspecification. First, the functional form of the estimated equation may be incorrect. If the data came from $Y = b_1 + b_2 X + b_3 X^2 + e$ and the equation $Y = b_1 + b_2 X + e$ is estimated, there will be systematic (autocorrelated) errors because of the failure of the estimated equation to take account of the real nonlinearity present. So one approach to the problem of serial correlation is to try different functional forms.

Another kind of misspecification arises when one omits important variables. If the equation produces systematic residuals (differences between forecast Y and actual Y), it may mean that some variable that both influences Y and moves systematically over time has been left out of the estimated equation. If alternative sensible functional forms don't get rid of the serial correlation, one might reconsider the basic independent variables being employed. Has something important been left out? If the answer is yes, the solution is to reestimate with the omitted variable or variables present.

In an attempt to explain and solve a problem of serial correlation, it is sometimes useful to look at a graph of the estimated residuals against time and see if a significant pattern is apparent. This is not generally productive, though, unless detailed knowledge of the sample period, not embodied in the data, is available. (Knowing in which years major wars took place is an example of information of this sort.) A graph of serially correlated residuals against time usually resembles a sine wave plus noise and is not especially informative.

Finally, if only Assumption 5 fails, so that the variance of the errors is not constant, least-squares estimates are still unbiased but not efficient. If you have some idea of how the variance of the errors changes from observation to observation, it is possible to transform the variables so that efficient estimates of the b's are obtained. The null hypothesis of equal variances, or *homoscedasticity,* can be tested against the alternative of unequal variances, *heteroscedasticity.*

Before examining the output produced by a multiple regression program, we must consider testing hypotheses on the true coefficients in (2-12). Under Assumption 6, that we have normally distributed errors, least-squares estimates of these coefficients are normally distributed with unknown variance. Suppose the standard deviation of $\hat{b}_i$ is estimated to be $\hat{\sigma}_i$ by the regression program. If the null hypothesis $b_i = Q$ is to be tested, the discussion in the last part of the last section suggests that the following statistic be employed:

$$t = (\hat{b}_i - Q)/\hat{\sigma}_i \tag{2-13}$$

This is the so-called t *statistic.* If the null hypothesis is true, it is distributed as Student's t with mean zero. If b_i is not equal to Q, the distribution of t will clearly *not* have mean zero.

Recalling the discussion in the last section, if $\hat{\sigma}_i$ were replaced in (2-13) by σ_i, the unknown true variance of $\hat{b}_i$, the null hypothesis would be rejected at the 5% level if t were above 1.96 or below −1.96. Similarly, absolute values of t in excess of 2.58 would serve to reject the null hypothesis at the 1% level. Since the σ_i are never known, we must consider the *degrees of freedom* of the regression. If there are T

observations and n coefficients, the regression is said to have $T-n$ degrees of freedom. The larger the number of degrees of freedom, intuitively, the more confident we can be of our estimate of σ_i, and the more nearly we can act as if this quantity were known for certain to be equal to our estimate.

In fact, unless T is at least equal to n, it is algebraically impossible to compute least-squares estimates. (As before, the computer will attempt to divide by zero and fail.) If T is equal to n, the estimated residuals will all be zero, and the $\hat{\sigma}_i$ will be zero also. (It is always possible to pass a straight line exactly through any two points in a plane, a plane can always be passed exactly through any three points in three dimensions, and so on.) It may seem hard to believe that the next observation encountered will be exactly explained by such an equation, or that simply because additional observations are not available we have found exactly the true coefficients. The larger is $T-n$, the more information available per coefficient.

The exact density function of the t statistic defined by (2-13), therefore, depends on the degrees of freedom of the regression, on the "quality" of the estimated coefficients and of their estimated standard deviations. For more than 20 degrees of freedom, t's larger that 2.09 in absolute value serve to reject the null hypothesis being tested at the 5% level. A t value of 2.85 signals rejection at the 1% level. If the regression involves fewer than 20 degrees of freedom, you must consult the tables in the references for the exact values of t that are needed to reject the null hypothesis.

Finally, it should be clear from our earlier discussion of the relation between confidence intervals and hypothesis testing, that the hypothesis $b_i = Q$ will be rejected at, say, the 5% level if and only if the 95% confidence interval for b_i does not include Q.

Regression: Interpretation of Results

Suppose we have gathered or been given a body of data, we have checked the situation being modeled to be sure that there are no obvious reasons to expect that any of Assumptions 1–5 are violated, and we have gone to the closest computer and estimated the coefficients of a plausible regression equation of the form of (2-2) that incorporates all the information we can distill from economic theory and common sense. We now must examine the statistics the computer provides to see what they can tell us about our trial equation.

The following are the main outputs of most regression programs:

1. Standard error of the regression
2. Estimated coefficients
3. Standard errors of the coefficients
4. t statistics
5. R^2 statistic
6. Durbin-Watson statistic

Let us discuss each of these in turn.

The *standard error of the equation,* or the *standard error of estimate,* is simply the estimated standard deviation of the error term, $\hat{\sigma}_e$ in our notation. Notice that the standard error obtained will depend on the exact dependent variable used. An equation with dependent variable Y will, in general, have a larger standard error than the same equation with log Y, as the dependent quantity. This is because the variance of Y is usually greater than the variance of log Y, since, for Y greater than one, Y is larger than its logarithm. The real significance of the standard error is how large it is relative to the variance of the actual dependent variable used, and this is measured, as we shall see, by the R^2 statistic.

The main use of the standard error, which we discuss below, is to provide an indication of the margin of error to be associated with forecasts made from estimated equations.

In terms of our notation, the *estimated coefficients* are the $\hat{b}_i$, and the *standard errors of the coefficients* are the $\hat{\sigma}_i$, the estimated standard deviations of the estimated coefficients. The *t statistics* are simply the ratios of the coefficients to their estimated standard errors. A glance at (2-13) indicates that the null hypothesis that the coefficient is zero is implicitly being tested. If the absolute value of the t statistic is large enough to reject this null hypothesis at, say, 5%, the coefficient is said to be significant at the 5% level.

If the coefficient also has the expected sign and a reasonable magnitude, there is a strong presumption that the corresponding independent variable does affect the dependent variable.

Besides the standard errors, most regression programs provide the *estimated variance-covariance matrix of the coefficients*. The $\hat{\sigma}_i$ are simply the square roots of the estimated variances. The estimated covariances can be used to test hypotheses and establish confidence intervals on linear combinations of the b's, that is, expressions of the form $c_1 b_1 + c_2 b_2 \ldots + c_n b_n$, where the c's are constants. The fundamental result that makes this possible is the following. If U and V are normally distributed random variables with mean μ_u and μ_v, variances σ_u^2 and σ_v^2, and covariance cov (u,v), the linear combination $aU + bV$, with a and b any constants, is normally distributed with mean $a\mu_u + b\mu_v$ and variance $a^2 \sigma^2{}_u + b^2 \sigma^2{}_v + 2ab$ cov (u,v). (This result underlies the statements made above about the distribution of $\hat{\mu}_x$ in normal populations.)

If, for example, it is desired to test the null hypothesis $b_1 = b_2$, the following t statistic is computed:

$$(\hat{b}_1 - \hat{b}_2)/\sqrt{\hat{\sigma}_1^2 + \hat{\sigma}_2^2 - 2 \widehat{\text{cov}} (\hat{b}_1, \hat{b}_2)}$$

All the quantities under the square-root sign are taken from the estimated variance-covariance matrix of the coefficients. There are still $T-n$ degrees of freedom associated with this statistic.

Since forecasts of Y from a model of the form of (2-12) are simply linear combinations of the b_i, an estimated variance of forecast can be computed following this sort of procedure, and confidence intervals on the actual value of the dependent variable can be calculated. If Y is the (unknown) actual value of the dependent variable being forecast, and $\hat{Y}$ is the forecast made from a regression equation, the estimated variance of forecast is an estimate of $E[(\hat{Y}-Y)^2]$. It can be shown to depend on the variance-covariance matrix of the coefficients, which in turn depends on $\hat{\sigma}_e$ and on the values of the X's which are used to generate $\hat{Y}$. The estimated variance is always greater than or equal to $\hat{\sigma}_e{}^2$.

The fifth item on the list above, the R^2 *statistic*, is a measure of how well the model explains the movements of the dependent variable. It is defined by the following equation:

$$R^2 = 1 - \frac{\sum\limits_{i=1}^{T} \hat{e}(t)^2}{\sum\limits_{i=1}^{T} [Y(t) - \hat{\mu}_Y]^2}$$

From this definition, it should be clear that least squares can be thought of as a procedure for maximizing R^2. The value of R^2 will always be between zero and one if the regression contains a constant term. It may be less than zero if no constant is present. R^2 is usually interpreted as the percentage of the variance of the dependent variable explained by the regression equation. (If you know about analysis of variance, this should sound familiar. Indeed, linear regression and analysis of variance are two ways of looking at the same statistical procedure.) The R^2 statistic is said to measure the *goodness of fit* of the regression. Remember, though, that econometrics is concerned with more than obtaining R^2's close to one. The individual coefficients must be siginificant and reasonable, and the form of the equation must be sensible.

The *F statistic,* which is provided by many regression programs, can be used to test for the significance of R^2. That is, it provides a test of the null hypothesis that all of the true b's are zero, that no relationship is present. If this hypothesis is true, then $[R^2/(n-1)]/[(1-R^2)/(T-n)]$ is distributed as F with $n-1$ and $T-n$ degrees of freedom. Large values of F serve to reject the null hypothesis. This is generally a weak test, especially in time-series analysis, since seemingly low values of R^2 are usually shown to be significant by the F test. If one desires to use this test, one must consult a table in the references or elsewhere.

The *Durbin-Watson (DW) statistic* is used to test the hypothesis that adjacent errors are uncorrelated. *This statistic is essentially worthless if lagged values of Y have been employed as independent variables in the regression.* Our discussion applies only to the case where no lagged dependent variables are present. The formal model that underlies the DW test considers the error term, $e(t)$, as having been generated by a process of the following sort:

$$e(t) = \rho e(t-1) + u(t)$$

where ρ is a constant between -1 and $+1$, and adjacent values of $u(t)$ are not correlated. This is called a first-order Markov process, and ρ is the first-order serial correlation coefficient.

If such a process is generating the e's, the expected value of the DW statistic is approximately $2(1-\rho)$; the range of the DW statistic is 0–4. Values of DW less than two indicate a ρ between zero and one. Looking at the equation above, this means that successive error terms will be close together. With a value of ρ of 0.90, for instance, one would expect a long run of positive errors followed by a long run of negative errors, and so on. The pattern of residuals against time would generally resemble (as mentioned above) a noisy sine wave. If ρ is between zero and -1, on the other hand, positive errors tend to be followed immediately by negative errors, and vice versa. The first case $(0 < p \leq +1)$ is called *positive serial correlation*, and the second situation $(-1 \leq p < 0)$ is referred to as *negative serial correlation*. Positive serial correlation is the more common of the two problems.

What values of the Durbin-Watson statistic serve to reject the null hypothesis of no first-order autocorrelation, the hypothesis $\rho = 0$? Naturally, the critical values depend on the number of observations and on the number of estimated coefficients (see the references for tables). The DW test has a rather bothersome peculiarity. The tables present values, labeled d_{ϱ}, such that the hypothesis of no serial correlation is rejected if DW is less than d_{ϱ} or greater than $4 - d_{\varrho}$. The tables also show another set of numbers, labeled d_u, such that the null hypothesis is retained if DW is between d_u and $4-d_u$. If DW is the range of $d_{\varrho}-d_u$ or $(4-d_u)-(4-d_{\varrho})$, nothing definite can be said. A safe course is to reject the null hypothesis if DW is outside the range $d_u-(4-d_u)$. A rough rule of thumb is that a value of DW outside the range 1.5–2.5 signals trouble.

REFERENCES

We have come to the end of our informal treatment of multiple regression. We have (hopefully) made no really incorrect statements, but neither have we verified most of what we've said. Listed below are some textbooks that can be read by students with no mathematics beyond elementary calculus which examine econometrics more rigorously than we have been able to do here. Many of the difficult points that we have glossed over are dealt with in these texts, useful tables are presented, and techniques beyond ordinary least-squares regression are developed. It is highly recommended that the student look at one or more of these books before attempting any actual estimation. The texts are arranged roughly in order of increasing difficulty.

Brennan, M. J., *Preface to Econometrics,* Second Edition, South-Western Publishing Co., Cincinnati, Ohio, 1965.

Klein, L. R., *An Introduction to Econometrics,* Prentice-Hall, Inc., Englewood Cliffs, New Jersey, 1962.

Kane, E. J., *Economic Statistics and Econometrics,* Harper & Row, Publishers, New York, 1968.

Walters, A. A., *An Introduction to Econometrics,* W. W. Norton & Company, Inc., New York, 1970.

Wonnacott, R. J., and T. H. Wonnacott, *Econometrics,* John Wiley & Sons, Inc., New York, 1970, Part I.

The books by Kane and by Wonnacott and Wonnacott contain fairly complete sets of tables, and the latter assumes a basic knowledge of statistics. The various editions of the CRC handbook of Standard Mathematical Tables contain tables for the F and t tests.

THE ESTIMATION EXERCISES

3

The nature of the estimation exercises may be
clarified a bit by a discussion of the sort of role-
playing you might engage in. Imagine that you're
on the headquarters staff of a large conglomerate, or
of the Council of Economic Advisors, or even of
Nader's Raiders. You want to investigate first the
demand structure and then the cost functions of a
particular industry. Your diligent staff has come up
with some historical information, which is described
in the next section. Your task is to intelligently use
these data and to present your conclusions in an
informative report. The main difference between
these exercises and real-world problems of the sort
described is that the data here are better and the
situation investigated is simpler than is usual in
reality.

The nature of your industry and of your data are discussed in the next section. The chapter's third section briefly presents commonly made mistakes in applied econometric work, such as you will be doing. It was kept short since experience suggests that you will learn more by using linear regression than by reading about its use. Scientific though economics tries to be, applied econometrics is still somewhat of an art. The final two sections of the chapter contain suggestions about the reports which you will write on these exercises and a short list of recommended readings.

The Industry Studied

All cost data refer to the operations of a typical firm in the industry under study. Similarly, the demand data refer to the demand experienced by an average firm in periods in which all firms were selling at the same price.

The population and the general price level (cost of living) remained constant in the period for which data are provided. Aggregate disposable income (consumer's income after taxes) did change, however, and you will be given the values it attained.

During the period for which data are provided, the industry was composed of a large number of firms, and the number of firms was the same in all years. (You will be given the number of firms in the forecasting problem; you do not need this fact here.) Each firm operated one plant producing a nondurable consumer good. All plants were and are identical, and all have a capacity of 100,000 units of output per year. No more can be produced under any circumstances. There has been no technical change in this industry; the same production process was used in all years for which data are provided.

The variable factors of production (such as labor of various skills and different raw materials) were and are used in strictly fixed proportions. An index of the price of these factors will be provided along with other cost data if these prices have changed over the period. (If homogeneous labor were the only variable factor, this index would be equal to the wage rate in each year divided by the wage rate in an arbitrary base year.) Cost figures include the opportunity cost of capital and entrepreneurship. Notice that the assumption of unchanged plants means that some factors of production were fixed throughout the period.

If this were all you knew about the industry, you would be faced with a rather severe problem. Price and quantity would be determined by the intersection of the industry supply and demand curves. Since disposable income and the prices of the variable factors of production varied over the period, both curves would be identified, as discussed in the last chapter. But any sensible model of the industry would have to take account of the fact that price and output were determined by two simultaneous equations. Ordinary least squares could not be used for your investigations, as it would produce asymptotically biased estimates, i.e., estimates that would differ systematically from the true coefficients no matter how many observations you had available. (This was discussed in the last chapter.)

One fact about the industry, stated in Chapter 1, makes it possible for you to apply ordinary linear regression. At no time in the past has the market price of the industry's output been determined wholly by supply and demand. The output of each firm in the industry was either determined directly by the government or fixed by arbitrary nonprice rationing of an essential input factor. Thus firms' costs did not affect supply or price; output was an exogenous variable. Since the market was not necessarily at the

intersection point of the supply and demand schedules at any time, it would be inappropriate to employ
a simultaneous-equations model. Least squares can be
used.

Estimating Economic Relationships

A first warning. When you are given a listing of data,
there is a natural tendency to pore over it in an
attempt to discover significant relationships. This is
generally harmless even if not too productive. But
many students waste hours trying to obtain simple
insights from a large number of figures. The computer
can summarize and analyze data better than you can
with a pencil and paper. Use the computer for what it
can do best.

This remark calls for a second caveat. The computer cannot think, and it knows no economic
theory. Since the number of equations you can
estimate will generally be limited, you must do some
analysis before going to the computer. The demand
function is a model of consumer decision-making, and
the cost function reflects both technology and
managerial choices. You must make sure that the
equations you estimate reflect these characteristics of
the underlying relationships. Are the right variables
present? Are the functional forms economically
sensible? Are they needlessly complex? You should
be certain that you have a good working knowledge
of cost and demand theory before beginning
estimation.

Do not try to use the computer to select "important" variables before estimating cost and demand
functions. When one variable depends on two or more
other variables, regressing the dependent variable on
the independent variables one-at-a-time can produce
highly misleading results. To dramatize this point,
consider the data presented in Table 3.1. Examine
first only the variables Z and X. Notice that exactly

Table 3.1   Some Illustrative Data

Year	Y	Change in Y	X	Change in X	Z	Change in Z
1	10		1		9	
2	15	+	7	+	8	−
3	13	−	8	+	5	−
4	14	+	7	−	7	+
5	12	−	3	−	9	+
6	13	+	6	+	7	−
7	14	+	4	−	10	+

half of the changes in X are associated with changes in Z in the opposite direction. No relation is apparent between X and Z. If only Y and Z are considered, exactly the same conclusion is reached. Yet an examination of all three columns reveals that Y is always exactly equal to the sum of X and Z. All relevant variables must be present in a regression equation if one is to make sensible judgments about the importance of any of them.

Another common mistake is to estimate identities or near identities. Total revenue does depend on price and output; it is identically equal to their product. Any equation with revenue as a dependent variable and price and quantity as independent variables will produce a good fit. If the logarithms of these quantities are used, the fit will be perfect. But the equation will have no meaning at all in either case. If the same variable is present on both sides of an estimated equation, either directly or implicitly via an identity, be certain that there is a good, theoretically sound reason for it to be there. It may be appropriate to express all quantities in a demand equation in per capita terms when population is changing, but it will never make sense to multiply all variables in a demand relation by the selling price of the good in question.

After you have estimated a few sensible equations in either problem, it is again time for thought. Are any of your original hypotheses concerning important variables refuted by the results of estimation? Are any new hypotheses suggested? (Recall the use of the DW statistic as a signal of misspecification.) There is a great temptation to pore over residuals to find a functional form that fits the data slightly better than the ones first employed. There is nothing fundamentally wrong with this, except that it violates the venerable principle of Occam's Razor. Whenever a simple model or theory performs as well as a more complicated one, the simpler form should be retained. This means that variables whose coefficients are not significant can sometimes be dropped from the equation in order to increase the degrees of freedom available.

A final reason for considering only simple functional forms is that you will be required to use your estimated relationships in calculations later. The more complex the function you choose, the more laborious will be your computations.

Thoughts on Reports

In writing up your investigations of the cost and demand structure, it is useful to recall the scenario sketched out at the start of the chapter. What would a good report resemble in that sort of situation? The answer is clear; your supervisor would want to know what you did, why you did it, and what conclusions your research led to.

Keeping this in mind, a good report might first discuss what economic theory has to say about the form of the cost or demand relation being estimated. On the basis of this reasoning, you could then present and defend the equations you estimated. The heart of the paper should in all probability consist of your selection and defense of your best estimate of the relation under study. Both economic and statistical properties should be considered.

Finally, the nature of the demand or cost structure you estimated might be discussed. The relevant demand elasticities could be computed and their implications examined qualitatively. (Since these elasticities are not usually constant, the average values of the dependent and independent variables are usually employed in such computations.) Note that the cost data are short-run figures (no change in plant), so nothing can be said about returns to scale in production. The value and behavior of such things as marginal cost, average variable cost, and average fixed cost might be discussed, however.

Empirical research is always judged on the basis of the quality of the economic and statistical analysis. Goodness of fit is a desirable property in any estimated relationship, but it is not usually the most important consideration.

REFERENCES

To anyone familiar with published econometric studies of costs and demand, the artificiality of the problems posed here is apparent. Most published studies in these areas, especially those appearing in the last 10 years, employ rather sophisticated economic theory and statistical techniques to circumvent various problems. Further, a variety of institutional considerations and data-availability constraints inevitably complicate the analysis. Still, there are a few places where the reader of this text may look for further guidance as he approaches his demand and cost analysis problems. Some of these follow, roughly in order of increasing difficulty.

Klein, L. R., *An Introduction to Econometrics*, Prentice-Hall, Inc., Englewood Cliffs, New Jersey, 1962, Chapters 2 (demand) and 3 (cost).

Stokes, C. J., *Managerial Economics*, Random House, Inc., New York, 1969, Chapters 3 (demand) and 4 (cost).

Mansfield, E., ed., *Elementary Statistics for Economics and Business*, W. W. Norton & Company, Inc., New York, 1969, Part 4.

Johnston, J., *Statistical Cost Analysis*, McGraw-Hill Book Company, New York, 1960.

COMPETITIVE AND MONOPOLY PRICING

4

This chapter derives and discusses the conditions for competitive and monopoly equilibrium in a variant of the usual timeless static model. Purely competitive and monopolistic market structures can be handled analytically because there is a determinate relation between the industry demand curve and the demand curve facing each individual firm. Under monopoly, the industry demand curve is the demand curve facing the single firm present. If the market is competitive, each firm takes the going price as given beyond its control, though of course all firms together can sell only as much as industry demand permits. The demand curve facing the individual competitive firm is horizontal (infinitely elastic) at the going price. Under oligopoly, when there are few sellers, the demand curve facing each firm depends on the expectations the firm has about its competitors' actions and reactions. In such a situation, few neat mathematical results are possible. We deal qualitatively with oligopoly in Chapter 6.

Three basic elements underlie our analysis in this chapter. First is the *industry demand curve*, which gives the number of units of output that the industry can sell at each and every price. Whether an industry is competitive or monopolized, this function gives the relation between price and total industry sales.

The second element is the set of *cost functions* of the plants in the industry. We assume that each plant chooses the factors of production it uses to produce any output level so as to minimize the total cost of production. Thus the cost curves we analyze give the minimum cost of producing any level of output (less than capacity) in a given plant. These curves depend on the technology of production and the conditions of factor supply. Throughout, we assume that the opportunity cost of the capital embodied in each plant is included in that plant's fixed cost.

Finally, we assume that each firm, be it monopolist or pure competitor, seeks to *maximize* its *profits*. This assumption can be defended on at least two grounds. First, it makes some sense a priori as a description of firms' motivations, or at least as a first approximation thereto. Second, the profit-maximization assumption works. It enables one to use the differential calculus to obtain testable predictions about firm behavior, and these predictions have historically proven useful in a wide variety of circumstances. Under competitive conditions, for instance, firms that do not maximize, consciously or unconsciously, will be less efficient than firms that do, and they will tend to be driven out of business. It therefore makes some sense to consider all firms in competitive industries as maximizers, regardless of their true motivations.

The next section presents the mathematical techniques employed in the remainder of the chapter. References listed at the end of the chapter go into these methods in more detail; our purpose here is simply to introduce the basic tools and concepts.

The chapter's third section discusses short-run equilibrium in monopoly and competitive situations. In the short run, by assumption, the number of plants in the industry is fixed.

The fourth section then analyzes long-run competitive and monopoly equilibria, when the number of plants can be changed. Throughout, we assume a constant technology and perfectly elastic supply curves of factors of production.

Basic Mathematical Techniques

Suppose some variable y is a function of another quantity x, according to $y = f(x)$. It is desired to choose x so as to maximize y. If $x=x^*$ maximizes y, it must be the case that $df/dx = 0$, where the derivative is evaluated at $x=x^*$, as you should recall from elementary calculus. That is, the vanishing of the first derivative is a *necessary condition* for a maximum; any point that is a maximum satisfies it.

This is not a *sufficient condition*, though. We cannot say that any point that satisfies $df/dx = 0$ maximizes y. If $f(x)$ is *convex* (resembles a soup bowl right side up), the first derivative will be zero at the minimum of the function. The function $f(x)$ must be *concave* (shaped like an upside-down soup bowl) when the first derivative vanishes for a maximum to be indicated. Also, there may be several points at which $df/dx = 0$ and the function is concave. Each of these corresponds to a *local maximum*, a point where y is larger than at all nearby points. The largest of these local maxima is the *global maximum*.

In the remainder of this discussion, we present necessary conditions for maximization in some economically interesting situations. We assume that the functions involved are shaped so that (1) these conditions do signal a maximum and (2) there is a unique point satisfying these conditions. That is, we assume that the sufficient conditions for a global maximum are satisfied; such sufficient conditions are presented in the references listed at the end of this chapter.

The basic problem in what is usually called *marginal analysis* is of the following sort. Suppose that a decision-maker has two activities under his control. Let x and y be the levels at which these activities are to be carried out. We denote the *benefits* from these activities as $B(x,y)$ and the *costs* as $C(x,y)$. The decision-maker seeks to maximize net benefits, B-C. The necessary conditions for a maximum, found by setting the first partial derivatives of B-C equal to zero, are

$$\partial B/\partial x = \partial C/\partial x \quad \text{and} \quad \partial B/\partial y = \partial C/\partial y \qquad (4\text{-}1)$$

That is, the *marginal benefits from each activity must equal its marginal cost*. [It should be clear that if Eqs. (4-1) indicate a negative value for x or y, the corresponding activity should not be undertaken.]

In the case of a firm, x and y could be the outputs of two products. Then benefits are total sales revenue, and costs are production cost. Equations (4-1) in this case are just the familiar equalities between marginal cost and marginal revenue.

For the government, x and y might be spending on aircraft inspection and on ground-control equipment and personnel, two methods of reducing the risk of air crashes. $C(x,y)$ would then simply be $x + y$, while $B(x,y)$ would be some measure of the value of the reduced risk brought about by various possible spending patterns.

A simple example can illustrate the use of conditions (4-1). Suppose that $B(x, y) = 4x + 6y$ while $C(x,y) = x^2 + y^2$. Setting the partial derivatives of B-C with respect to x and y equal to zero yields

$$4 - 2x = 0 \quad \text{and} \quad 6 - 2y = 0$$

Solving, we have $x = 2$ and $y = 3$. Consideration of the shape of the function B-C should convince you that it is indeed maximized at this point.

An interesting special case of this problem is the following. Suppose there is only one output of interest, x. Benefits are a function of the amount of x produced. Suppose further that x can be produced two ways. Let x_1 be the amount produced the first way, and let $C^1(x_1)$ be the corresponding cost function. Similarly, the second method has output x_2 and cost function $C^2(x_2)$, with total output $x = x_1 + x_2$. Setting the first derivatives of B-$C^1 - C^2$ equal to zero, we obtain the necessary conditions.

$$\partial B/\partial x_1 = \partial B/\partial x = \partial C^1/\partial x_1$$

$$\partial B/\partial x_2 = \partial B/\partial x = \partial C^2/\partial x_2 \qquad (4\text{-}2)$$

These equations imply that the *marginal cost of producing the output must be the same for all techniques employed.*

This means, for instance, that a firm operating several plants should operate them so that the marginal cost of production is equal for all plants actually used. This is an *efficiency condition* for production, in the sense that no matter how much x is produced, if it is produced at minimum cost the marginal costs of all plants or methods employed must be equal. (If some methods or plants have marginal costs that are too high for this condition to be met at a given output level, those methods or plants should obviously not be used.)

So far, we have not explicitly considered any constraints on the levels of the activities of interest, though we have mentioned that usually the activities must be carried on at nonnegative levels. Suppose now that we have two activities x and y, and that these must be carried on so that the *constraint equation* $f(x,y) = k$ is satisfied, where k is some constant. This constraint could represent, for instance, the amount of money a household has available for the purchase of two commodities, x and y. The constraint equation would then take the form $P_x x + P_y y = k$, where the P's are the prices of x and y.

In order to maximize B-C subject to the constraint equation $f(x,y) = k$, we can employ a useful technique developed by Lagrange. Write down the *Lagrangian* expression

$$L = B(x,y) - C(x,y) + \lambda[k - f(x,y)]$$

Notice that the quantity in brackets must be zero. Necessary conditions for a maximum are that the first derivatives of L with respect to x, y, and the *Lagrangian multiplier*, λ, be zero. Formally, these conditions are

$$(\partial B/\partial x) - (\partial C/\partial x) - \lambda(\partial f/\partial x) = 0$$

$$(\partial B/\partial y) - (\partial C/\partial y) - \lambda(\partial f/\partial y) = 0 \qquad (4\text{-}3)$$

$$k - f(x,y) = 0$$

These three equations serve to determine the three unknowns, x, y, and λ. It can be shown that, if the functions involved are such that (4-3) does signal a maximum, λ is the derivative of B-C with respect to k. That is, λ measures the marginal value of increasing k. In many economic applications, k is the amount of some fixed resource available to the decision-maker, and λ can be interpreted as the marginal value of that resource. If there are two such resources, there will be two constraints, two multipliers, and so on.

Let us illustrate the use of conditions (4-3) by a slight extension of our earlier example. We wish to maximize

$$B(x,y) - C(x,y) = 4x + 6y - x^2 - y^2$$

but now we assume that x and y must satisfy the constraint equation

$$x + y = k$$

Here the Lagrangian is

$$L = 4x + 6y - x^2 - y^2 + \lambda(k - x - y)$$

Differentiating, we find the three equations corresponding to conditions (4-3) to be

$$4 - 2x - \lambda = 0$$

$$6 - 2y - \lambda = 0$$

$$k - x - y = 0$$

For $k = 1$, the solution to this system of three equations in three unknowns is easily seen to be $x = 0$, $y = 1$, and $\lambda = 4$. If the constant k were the available input of some resource costing \$3.50 per unit, and if the maximand were dollar profit, the value of λ indicates that a small additional purchase of the resource in question would be worthwhile. For $k = 2$, the solution to the three equations above is $x = 1/2$, $y = 3/2$, and $\lambda = 3$. At this point, additional purchases at a price of \$3.50 would not be profitable.

Suppose that k were equal to 10. We showed above that the unconstrained maximum of B-C occurred at

$x = 2$, $y = 3$. If k represents the available quantity of a scarce resource, the decision-maker will never use more than five units unless he is forced to. This leads to consideration of a more general problem, where the constraints take the form of inequalities rather than equalities.

Consider maximizing B-C subject to the *constraint inequality* $f(x,y) \leq k$. If the constraint involves a scarce resource, this inequality says that the decision-maker may employ up to k units of the resource, but he need not use all k units available. For example, k might be the maximum possible output of a plant. Problems of this sort may be solved by using the *Kuhn-Tucker theorem*. To employ this technique we proceed as above to form the Lagrangian and then differentiate, as before, to obtain the first two of conditions (4-3). Those two equations are necessary conditions for this more general problem. The Kuhn-Tucker theorem then says that one and only one of the following conditions must hold.

(a) $f(x,y) < k$ and $\lambda = 0$

(b) $f(x,y) = k$ and $\lambda > 0$

In case (a), the constraint is said to be not binding, and the marginal value of the fixed resource in question is zero. It would not pay the decision-maker to purchase additional units of the resource, since he maximizes B-C without using the full amount already available. In case (b), the constraint is said to be *binding*. Additional units of fixed resource do have positive value. (Whether this value is greater than the cost of the resource is, of course, another question.) In any real-world problem, the solution will be either of form (a) or form (b). It is possible in theory to have $f(x,y) = k$ and $\lambda = 0$, but this almost never happens in practice. In the numerical example discussed above, if the constraint is $x + y \leq k$, case (a) can easily be seen to apply whenever k is greater than five. Only for k exactly equal to five do we have $\lambda = 0$ and $x + y = k$.

In simple situations trial and error may be employed to find the solution. One might assume that case (a) obtains and solve for x and y with $\lambda = 0$. If the constraint is satisfied, the problem is solved. If not, assume that case (b) holds and find a solution in which $f(x,y) = k$. With one or two constraints, the trial and error process is not difficult.

When there are N constraints, each of which may or may not be binding, there are 2^N possible cases of this sort to be considered. When N is larger than two or three, the computation involved in trial and error searches for the right combination of binding and nonbinding constraints becomes too involved. In such cases, the techniques of mathematical programming are used to obtain solutions without resorting to trial and error. The simplex method for linear programming is the best-known such procedure; it can be used when the functions B and C and all the constraint inequalities are linear functions of the activity levels.

This short section has presented a lot of material in a superficial way. For our purposes here and in the next chapter, this treatment is hopefully adequate. The references at the end of the chapter cover these topics in more depth; the interested (or confused) reader should examine them.

Short-run Equilibrium

Standard price theory tells us that a competitive firm sets output so that price equals marginal cost, while a monopolist equates marginal revenue and marginal cost. In the short run, if a competitive industry and a monopolist have the same plants available, the monopolist will produce less and earn larger profits than the competitive industry. The community is generally better off under competition.

In this section, we apply the mathematical tools just presented to the determination of competitive and monopoly pricing. Our aim is to develop the methods needed to solve the forecasting problems of the next chapter. Accordingly, we make some simplifying assumptions which are also made there. First, we assume that the prices of the factors of production and raw materials used by the industry do not depend on the industry's output. This is the assumption of *perfectly competitive factor markets*. We suppose the industry considered to be only a small purchaser (relative to the relevant markets) of the factors of production it uses.

Secondly, we assume that the industry is composed of N *identical plants*. With no changes in technology, this is a reasonable assumption. If there is a best sort of plant, all plants built will be of this type. If there is no best plant, all plants will be identical by definition. The term *plant* must be interpreted broadly in this context; an optimal plant may consist of one machine, one man, and 100 square feet of floor space with a roof over it. Then a plant in the usual sense would consist of a number of these plants at the same location.

Let q be the output, measured in physical, not value units, of a typical plant, and write the cost function of a typical plant as $C(q)$. We denote the short-run marginal cost of production in the typical plant as $MC(q)$. By definition, $MC(q) = dC/dq$, the derivitive of total cost with respect to output. We assume that no plant can produce more than k units of output in any period, and we refer to k as capacity output. (If there is no upper limit on output on the short run, k can be made very large so that the capacity constraint in what follows is never binding.)

Denote the industry's total demand by Q and the price at which these sales are made by P. These two quantities are connected by the industry demand relation $P = P(Q)$, with $dP/dQ < 0$. We examine short-run equilibrium under these assumptions, first for a competitive industry and then for a monopoly.

As long as there are a large number of firms and the market is perfectly competitive, it does not matter how many plants each firm owns. Each plant will be operated so as to maximize the profit it earns, on the assumption that the firm's activities will not alter the market price because any one firm is only a minute part of the industry. Thus each plant in the industry will be operated so as to maximize the difference between revenue and cost:

$$Pq - C(q) \tag{4-4}$$

where P is treated as a parameter beyond the control of the firm—in particular, P is constant regardless of the value of q chosen. The quantity (4-4) must be maximized subject to the constraint $q \leq k$.

We first solve the problem algebraically. As in the last section, we form the relevant Lagrangian

$$L = Pq - C(q) + \lambda(k - q) \tag{4-5}$$

From the discussion in the last section, the first necessary condition for maximum profits is found by differentiating the Lagrangian with respect to q, treating P as a constant. Using the Kuhn-Tucker theorem, the set of necessary conditions is

$P - MC(q) - \lambda = 0 \qquad$ and either

$(a) \quad q = k \quad$ and $\quad \lambda > 0 \quad$ or $\tag{4-6}$

$(b) \quad q < k \quad$ and $\quad \lambda = 0$

For any given value of P, we can solve these conditions for the output of a typical plant. Note that P will equal MC unless P is greater than $MC(k)$, marginal cost at capacity output. For prices greater than this value, all plants in the industry will produce capacity output. The multiplier λ measures the amount by which profits would rise if k were increased, since $P - MC(k)$ is the profit that would be earned on the next unit of output. If optimal q is less than k, it is clear that λ should be zero.

Now that we know how firms' supplies vary with market price, it is a rather simple matter to determine industry equilibrium. Suppose that we have solved conditions (4-6) for q as a function of P. Call this function $q^s(P)$; this is the short-run supply curve of a typical plant. Then, since there are N identical plants present, $Nq^s(P)$ is the industry's short-run supply schedule. Solving the industry demand function for Q, we can write it as $Q = Q^d(P)$. In equilibrium, supply equals demand, so we have

$$Nq^s(P) = Q^d(P) \tag{4-7}$$

This equation can be solved for P, since N is given. Once P is known, Q and $q(=Q/N)$ can be calculated from the demand schedule.

The steps in this solution process are really quite simple. First find out how much the typical profit-maximizing plant would supply at each price. Then multiply by N to obtain the industry's supply as a function of price. Finally, the intersection of this function with the industry demand curve is used to determine equilibrium price and output.

In practice, one can skip much of this procedure. The entire industry supply curve need not be derived, since one is usually interested only in the supply–demand intersection point. This can be obtained by substituting $P(Nq)$, the demand function, for P in (4-6) and solving for q. We shall illustrate this below.

We can further clarify the nature of the short-run equilibrium by considering Figure 4.1. This graph refers to a single plant, where we define $q^d(P) = Q^d(P)/N$. This curve shows what market price

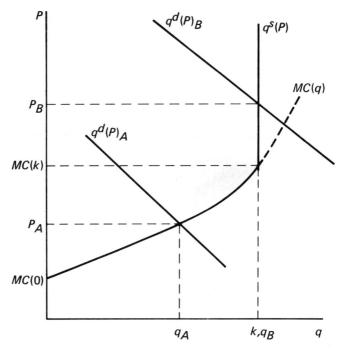

Figure 4.1   Short-run competitive equilibrium.

would be if all plants produced identical outputs or, equivalently, it shows how much each plant would sell if all plants charged the same price. (Recall the demand relation estimated in the last chapter.) It is *not* the demand curve relevant to the plants' decisions, since each plant is assumed so small relative to the industry that its output cannot in any way affect that of its competitors. But q^d must equal q^s *in equilibrium*; supply must equal demand, and the market must clear.

Suppose that the industry demand function and the number of plants are such that $q^d(P)_A$ applies to each plant. At equilibrium, price is equal to marginal cost, and output is below capacity. Were demand to shift to $q^d(P)_B$, price could not equal marginal cost.

The q^d and MC curves intersect only for an output above capacity. Clearly, a rational firm will produce all it can, k, and the market price will settle at P_B. In the first of these cases, the multiplier λ in (4-6) will be zero, while in the second, with a larger demand and capacity output being produced, the multiplier will be positive. Since price is above marginal cost in the second case, another unit of capacity would be profitable for each firm individually, though the industry as a whole might lose profits if more capacity were purchased.

The methods of analysis used when the industry is monopolized are the same as those employed above for perfect competition, with one major difference. The monopolist is assumed to be correctly aware that his production decision will fix the market price. He is still interested in maximizing the difference between revenue and cost; however, he must treat the market price, not as a parameter, but as a variable which he determines.

We assume, as above, there are N identical plants in the industry, but now all are under the control of a single firm. Since the plants are identical, they will each produce the same amount under any rational plan. Thus we can assume $q = Q/N$ here as under competition. (If the plants were not identical, cost-minimizing production would require that all plants actually operated have the same marginal cost; see the last section.)

Using the same notation as above, the monopolist is trying to maximize his profit

$$P(Q)Q - NC(Q/N) \tag{4-8}$$

subject to the constraint $Q/N \le k$. The relevant Lagrangian is

$$L = P(Q)Q - NC(Q/N) + \lambda[k - (Q/N)] \tag{4-9}$$

Since N is fixed in the short run, the necessary conditions become simply

$$[P + Q(dP/dQ)] - MC(Q/N) - (\lambda/N) = 0$$
and either

(a) $Q/N = k$ and $\lambda > 0$ or

(b) $Q/N < k$ and $\lambda = 0$

(4-10)

The quantity in brackets in the first of these conditions is simply the derivative of total revenue with respect to output, the monopolist's *marginal revenue*. Since it varies along the demand curve, marginal revenue is clearly a function of output, Q. To clarify our formulas, we thus define

$$MR(Q) = P(Q) + QdP(Q)/dQ$$

Then the first of conditions (4-10) becomes

$$MR(Q) - MC(Q/N) - (\lambda/N) = 0 \qquad (4\text{-}11)$$

Condition (4-10) states that marginal revenue must equal marginal cost if plants are not producing capacity output. If capacity output is produced, then marginal revenue must be above marginal cost. Notice that if "marginal revenue" is replaced by "price" in the last two sentences, they become the conditions for a short-run competitive equilibrium. Marginal revenue will be less than price at all output levels, since dP/dQ is negative, so price will always be above marginal cost for the monopolist. Since marginal cost is always positive, marginal revenue must also be positive at equilibrium. It is easy to show that this means that industry demand must be elastic at monopoly equilibrium. It should also be noted that a monopolist's production decision depends not only on price, but also on the rate of change of price with respect to output, dP/dQ. Thus a monopolist has no supply curve; the quantity he will supply to the market depends on the whole demand curve.

In any particular problem, the path from condition (4-10) to a solution is rather short. One first seeks a solution of (4-10) with $\lambda = 0$. If this solution satisfies $Q/N < k$, plant and firm output have been found. If not, it must be the case that $Q/N = k$, maximum per plant output. Once output has been determined, the industry's demand function yields the price at which this output can be sold.

As in the competitive case, we now proceed to present the solution for a typical plant graphically. For a fixed number of plants, we can write marginal revenue as $MR(Nq)$, where, as before, q is the output of a typical plant. We write the demand relation as $P = P(Nq)$. (Solving this equation for q, we would obtain $q = q^d(P)$, the function discussed in the competitive case.)

Now consider Figure 4.2. The cost structure for a typical plant is represented by the curve giving short-run marginal cost as a function of output. If the demand structure is such that $P(Nq)_A$ applies, the solution is the usual textbook one. Each plant will produce q_A, the firm will produce Nq_A, and price will be P_A. Marginal cost is equal to marginal revenue. Under demand regime B marginal revenue is above marginal cost, and all plants are producing capacity output.

A simple example will illustrate the calculation of short-run equilibria. Suppose industry demand is given by

$$P(Q) = 70 - 0.01Q$$

while each plant's marginal cost function is

$$MC(q) = 10 + q$$

(We do not need to know fixed cost to determine

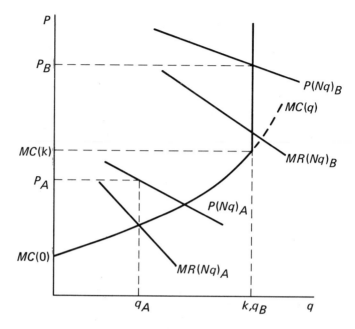

Figure 4.2   Short-run monopoly equilibrium.

short-run equilibria.) Assume that capacity, k, is 25 and that N, the number of plants, is 100.

Substituting $100q$ for Q in the demand function, and substituting the demand function for P in conditions (4-6) for competitive equilibrium, these become

$$(70 - q) - (10 + q) - \lambda = 0 \quad \text{and either}$$

$(a) \quad q = 25 \quad \text{and} \quad \lambda > 0 \quad \text{or}$

$(b) \quad q < 25 \quad \text{and} \quad \lambda = 0$

Let us first see if case (b) holds. Assuming $\lambda = 0$, we solve the equation in q and λ and obtain $q = 30$. This is not less than 25, so case (a) must hold. When $q = 25$, and all plants are operating at capacity, the equation yields $\lambda = 10$, which is positive as required. Industry output is thus 2500, and, from the demand function, price is 45.

To find the monopoly equilibrium position, we first note that the assumed demand function yields

$$MR(Q) = 70 - 0.02Q$$

Substituting, conditions (4-10) become

$$(70 - 0.02Q) - [10 + (Q/100)] - (\lambda/100) = 0$$
and either

(a) $Q/100 = 25$ and $\lambda > 0$ or
(b) $Q/100 < 25$ and $\lambda = 0$

We first examine case (a). If $Q/100 = 25$, or $Q = 2500$, the equation in Q and λ yields $\lambda = -1500$. Since this is negative, case (a) cannot hold. Setting $\lambda = 0$ as is appropriate for case (b), we find $Q = 2000$. This yields $q = 20$ and, from the demand function, $P = 50$.

Long-run Equilibrium

In the long run, both the kind and number of plants in an industry can change. Were we to simply add more variables and functions and mechanically proceed to derive necessary conditions, the results would convey little insight. We must make additional assumptions in order to obtain results useable in the next chapter's exercises.

First, we strengthen the assumption of identical plants and assume that any new plant built must be identical to the plants presently operating. Further, we assume that there are no economies or diseconomies of multiplant operations. We can thus write the cost of efficiently producing output Q in N plants as

$$NC(Q/N)$$

as in the last section. This expression is the same one employed in the short-run analysis, but now N may vary.

The long-run equilibrium condition for a monopolist is the same as the short-run condition: the firm will maximize its profits. In the long run, though, the number of plants it operates is under its control. Firms in a competitive industry will also try to maximize profits in the long run as in the short run, but we assume totally free entry into and exit from the competitive industry. This means that the profits earned by each plant, though they are being maximized, must be zero in long-run equilibrium. Positive profits would attract new firms; losses would force some firms to leave the industry. (As usual, by profits we mean economic profits, i.e., earnings in excess of opportunity cost.)

The short-run equilibria derived in the last section were characterized by relations between price and marginal cost under competition and between marginal revenue and marginal cost under monopoly. There we were considering short-run marginal cost, the incremental cost of increasing output from a given plant or set of plants. Here one might expect to encounter equations relating long-run marginal cost to price and to marginal revenue. Long-run marginal cost should be the incremental cost of adding to output when the possibility of varying the number of plants is taken into account.

Since there is only one equilibrium condition (maximum profits) to worry about in the case of monopoly, we consider that situation first. We begin by treating the number of plants, N, as a continuous variable. Later we shall deal with the case where N

must be an integer. Given the capacity constraint, the Lagrangian for this problem is

$$L = P(Q)Q - NC(Q/N) + \lambda[k - (Q/N)] \qquad (4\text{-}12)$$

Differentiating with respect to Q and with respect to N, we have the necessary conditions for a maximum:

$$MR(Q) - MC(Q/N) - (\lambda/N) = 0$$
$$-C(Q/N) + (Q/N)MC(Q/N) + (\lambda/N)(Q/N) = 0$$

and either $\qquad\qquad\qquad\qquad\qquad\qquad (4\text{-}13)$

(a) $\quad Q/N < k \quad$ and $\quad \lambda = 0 \quad$ or

(b) $\quad Q/N = k \quad$ and $\quad \lambda > 0$

Consider case (a) first. Write $q = Q/N$. Then the second of conditions (4-13) becomes

$$C(q)/q = MC(q) \qquad (4\text{-}14)$$

That is, marginal cost must equal average cost if all plants are operated below capacity. It is well known (and easy to show) that when marginal cost equals average cost, average cost is at its minimum point. Thus where the typical plant has minimum average cost occurring at a level of output below capacity, each plant will be operated at that level of output. This sort of cost structure is illustrated by Figure 4.3(a). The minimum value of average total cost is labeled long-run marginal cost, *LRMC*, since it represents the total cost (including the cost of capacity) of producing an additional unit of output as cheaply as possible. In long-run equilibrium, each of the monopolist's plants will produce an output q^*.

If average cost is above marginal cost for all q less than or equal to k, Eq. (4-14) cannot be satisfied for any feasible output. The second of conditions (4-13) then implies that λ is positive. Thus case (b) applies, and q must equal k. (If average cost is minimized for

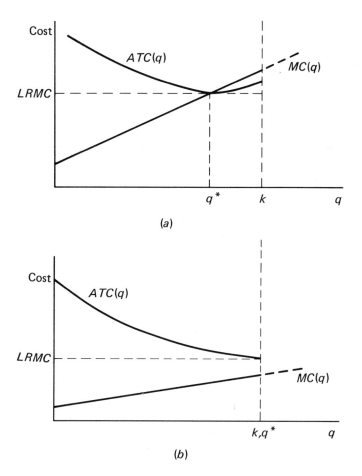

Figure 4.3 Long-run marginal cost: (*a*) minimum average total cost occurs at $q^* < k$; (*b*) minimum average total cost occurs at $q^* = k$.

$q = k$, we have the unlikely razor's edge case mentioned in the second section of this chapter. The constraint is just binding, but the multiplier, λ, is zero.) Case (*b*) is depicted in Figure 4.3(*b*). If average cost exceeds marginal cost for all q less than or equal to k or, equivalently, if average cost is falling for all feasible outputs, all the monopolist's plants will be operated at full capacity in long-run equilibrium.

Having used the second and third of conditions (4-13) to find output per plant in long-run equilibrium, we now use the first condition in order to obtain the optimal number of plants—and thus total firm output. Solve the second condition for λ/N, and substitute into the first. This yields

$$MR(Q) = C(Q/N)/(Q/N)$$

or marginal revenue equals average cost. Since we showed above that each plant will be operated at the output level q^* that minimizes average total cost, this equation may be rewritten as

$$MR(Nq^*) = C(q^*)/q^* \qquad (4\text{-}15)$$

which may be solved for N. Price is then obtained by substituting output, Nq^*, into the demand function, and the complete solution has been found.

This final step is illustrated by Figure 4.4. There Q_M is the monopolist's output, and P_M is his price. Division of Q_M by q^* yields the optimal number of plants.

Notice that in both cases (a) and (b) all output has been produced by running each plant at its most efficient level. We divided the solution into two parts: finding that level and computing the optimal number of plants. *If N is continuous, the long-run marginal cost of the monopolist is constant and equal to the minimum value of average total cost for the typical plant. Setting long-run marginal cost equal to marginal revenue yields the optimal quantity and thus the optimal number of plants.*

When N must be an integer, one more step must be performed. Suppose the above analysis gives N as 79.34. Then the optimal number of plants will be either 79 or 80. The procedure at this point is to

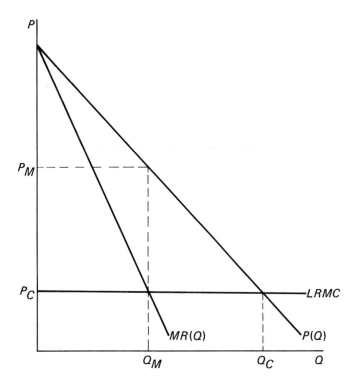

Figure 4.4 Long-run equilibria.

assume $N = 79$ and solve the short-run problem, do the same for $N = 80$, and choose that N for which profit is larger.

Consider, for instance, a monopoly with marginal cost and demand functions as in the example of the last section. The total cost function giving rise to the marginal cost schedule shown there must be of the form

$$TC(q) = 10q + (q^2/2) + FC$$

where FC is fixed cost. Suppose FC is 300. Then average total cost is

$$ATC(q) = 10 + (q/2) + (300/q)$$

It is easy to show that the derivative of average total cost with respect to q is negative for q less than or equal to capacity output of 25 units. Case (b) in conditions (4-13) thus applies, and if N were continuous, we would know that the monopolist would have all his plants producing capacity output, 25 units.

We now employ equation (4-15) to complete the solution. When $q = q^* = 25$, average total cost is easily seen to be 34.5. Equating this to marginal revenue yields

$$70 - 0.02N(25) = 34.5$$

which implies $N = 71$. Thus $Q = 1775$, and, from the demand function, $P = 52.25$. [Since (4-15) yielded an integer N, we did not have to compute and compare short-run equilibria for adjacent integer values.]

Let us now turn to the competitive situation. It is simplest here to work with a single plant and to use $q = Q/N$ (= the output of the plant) as our main variable. The plant owner or manager is assumed to maximize his profits; his Lagrangian is

$$L = Pq - C(q) + \lambda(k - q) \tag{4-16}$$

which is Eq. (4-5).

Since P is beyond the control of any single firm, the necessary conditions for maximum profit are simply conditions (4-6), which we rewrite here for convenience:

$$P - MC(q) - \lambda = 0 \qquad \text{and either}$$

$$(a) \quad q < k \quad \text{and} \quad \lambda = 0 \quad \text{or} \tag{4-17}$$

$$(b) \quad q = k \quad \text{and} \quad \lambda > 0$$

Given P, these conditions determine q. There are, however, three unknowns here, P, q, and N, and we need two more equations relating them.

The first of these is simply the demand function, which we can write as $P = P(nq)$. The third equation is provided by the condition that in long-run equilibrium with costless and unimpeded entry and exit, profits (in excess of opportunity cost) must be zero. Thus our third equation is

$$Pq - C(q) = 0 \qquad\qquad (4\text{-}18)$$

We could simply solve these equations on the assumption that case (b) held. If we find $\lambda > 0$ so that this assumption is verified, we have a solution. If not, case (a) must hold, and the equations that result when $\lambda = 0$ can be mechanically solved. But there is a way of looking at these equilibrium conditions that yields more insight.

Suppose case (a) applies. Then (4-17) and (4-18) imply

$$P = MC(q) = C(q)/q$$

That is, marginal cost equals average cost, and average cost must be, as we noted above, at its minimum point. If this equation does not hold for any q less than or equal to k, average cost must reach its minimum at capacity output, and case (b) will apply. We have found, perhaps not too surprisingly, just what we found for the monopoly case: industry output will be produced by operating each plant in the industry at the point where average total cost is minimized. *The long-run supply curve of the industry is flat when N is continuous, and it is equal to the minimum value of average total cost. Industry output is determined by setting long-run supply equal to demand.* As in the monopoly case, output per plant is determined only by the plant cost function, and the number of plants is determined by demand conditions.

Thus Figure 4.3 applies to both monopoly and competition. In both cases illustrated there, a competitive industry will have all plants operating at $q = q^*$ in long-run equilibrium. The long-run marginal cost is to be understood as the *industry's* long-run marginal cost; the industry supply curve will be horizontal at this value. Figure 4.4 illustrates the determination of the number of plants. When the value of $LRMC$ is substituted into the industry's demand equation, competitive output, Q_C, is determined. Division of Q_C by q^* yields the equilibrium number of plants, N. Figure 4.4 illustrates the fact that the monopoly will produce less than the competitive industry, even in the long run, and charge a higher price for its output.

Division of Q_C by q^* will usually not yield an integer. If the number of plants must be an integer, the procedure is again quite simple. If the analysis above yields $N = 34.8$, this means that 34 plants would each make a small profit, but 35 plants would lose money. Then the industry is in equilibrium with 34 plants present, as there is then no incentive to enter or leave the industry. The short-run equilibrium solution with $N = 34$ then yields q and P.

Let us illustrate the computation of long-run competitive equilibrium by considering an industry characterized by the marginal cost and demand functions employed above. Suppose now, though, that fixed cost is 200. Then, referring back to our computation of long-run monopoly equilibrium, each plant's average total cost is given by

$$ATC(q) = 10 + (q/2) + (200/q)$$

It can easily be verified that the function is minimized for $q = 20$. Thus case (a) in conditions

(4-17) applies, and the multiplier λ is zero. Equation (4-18) then yields $P = ATC(20) = 30$. We can then solve for N from the demand relation:

$$30 = 70 - 0.01N(20)$$

from which $N = 200$. As this is an integer, the solution is complete.

It must be emphasized that the nature of our long-run solutions depends rather heavily upon our assumptions. The most critical of these is that a monopolist owning N plants does not incur any additional costs or realize any savings because he operates more than one plant. (By way of contrast, the assumption that there is an optimal plant size is not overly important, since if there does not exist an optimal scale, N need not be integer.) The analytical devices we have employed can be applied to more complex situations, however, and if the reader has gained some insight into their use, this chapter has been successful.

REFERENCES

The economic concepts employed in this chapter are fairly standard and are developed in most intermediate-level price-theory texts. On the other hand, the maximization techniques developed and employed here, especially the Kuhn-Tucker theorem, are not commonly encountered in such texts. The following references, arranged roughly in increasing order of difficulty, discuss these mathematical tools.

Baumol, W. J., *Economic Theory and Operations Analysis*, Third Edition, Prentice-Hall, Inc., Englewood Cliffs, New Jersey, 1972, Chapters 4 and 7.

Enthoven, A. C., "The Simple Mathematics of Maximization," Appendix to C. J. Hitch and R. N. McKean, *The Economics of Defense in the Nuclear Age*, Atheneum Publishers, New York, 1965.

Naylor, T. H., and J. M. Vernon, *Microeconomics and Decision Models of the Firm,* Harcourt Brace Jovanovich, Inc., New York, 1969, Chapters 2 and 6 and the Mathematical Appendix to Chapter 2.

Intriligator, M. D., *Mathematical Optimization and Economic Theory,* Prentice-Hall, Inc., Englewood Cliffs, New Jersey, 1971, Chapters 2–4.

Hadley, G., *Nonlinear and Dynamic Programming,* Addison-Wesley Publishing Co., Inc., Reading, Massachusetts, 1964, Chapters 1–3 and 6.

THE FORECASTING PROBLEMS

5

Let us extend the scenario outlined at the start of Chapter 3. The industry you are studying was characterized by very low seller concentration in the past. Each plant was and is owned by a separate firm. Collusion to fix price and output is illegal and has never occurred, and there has never been a very effective trade association. The government is going to remove its output controls from this market, and part of your job is to forecast what will happen if the industry remains competitive.

There is a small chance that the plants currently in the industry will be purchased by a single firm before the government controls are removed. Your employer, who is considering buying the existing plants or suing the firm that does buy them all, depending on your taste, is quite interested in what would happen under this circumstance. You as a citizen are interested in the loss society would suffer if a monopoly were formed.

The next section describes both the data you will have available to perform these analyses and the methods to be used. We then discuss the problems in some detail. The chapter concludes with some brief suggestions about the report that you will write about your work.

Data and Methods

In the second exercise described in Chapter 3, you estimated the cost function of a typical plant. Total cost depended on output, factor prices, and perhaps other variables. The values of all variables exogenous to the industry will be given for this exercise, so it should be quite simple to convert your estimate into a total cost function that depends only on plant output. This cost function applies to each plant in the industry, regardless of the number of plants present. In the notation of the previous chapter, you should be able to convert your cost estimate into $C(q)$.

You will also be given the values for all exogenous variables that appear in your estimated demand equation. Substituting these in, you will obtain $q = q^d(P)$, in the notation of the last chapter. You will be told the number of plants, N_0, historically and currently present in the industry. Your estimate of the industry demand curve should then be

$$Q = N_0 q^d(P)$$

This function describes the demand for the industry's output regardless of how that output is produced, since doubling N_0 would merely halve $q^d(P)$ for all P.

Thus the values of the exogenous variables appearing in your demand and cost estimates plus the value of N_0 should enable you to obtain the functions used

THE FORECASTING PROBLEMS 77

in the last chapter's analysis. The tools and methods developed there can be directly applied to the problems discussed below.

Most of these problems involve the solution of simultaneous equations. If you have estimated simple cost and demand curves, this should be no great chore. In many cases, the function that provides the best fit to the data is considerably more complex than another equation which fits almost as well. Where the simpler function makes the algebra easier, use it. If analytical solution is difficult for all sensible demand and cost functions available, it may be possible to obtain approximate solutions graphically.

The Problems

Your first problem is to forecast the short-run equilibrium market price and the corresponding output per plant in your industry, given the values taken on by the exogenous variables. (Remember that each plant can produce a maximum of 100,000 units.) Then evaluate the profits earned by each plant and deduce whether or not the competitive industry would be in long-run equilibrium under these conditions.

If the industry is not in long-run equilibrium, would you expect firms to enter or leave it? You should compute the long-run equilibrium number of plants in the industry. (Note that the industry is in equilibrium with N plants if that number can earn a small excess profit but $N + 1$ plants would suffer losses.) What are the equilibrium values of price and output per plant?

Now suppose that all of the plants are owned by a single firm. Forecast the price that this monopolist will charge in the short run and the amount he will produce in an average plant. Evaluate total profits and profits per plant.

You should then consider whether the monopolist is in long-run equilibrium. Would he make more money with more or fewer plants? If the monopolist is not in long-run equilibrium, calculate the number of plants that would be present in long-run equilibrium. Compute the long-run equilibrium price and profit, and output per plant of a monopolist.

In both short-run and long-run equilibrium, you should find that the monopolist would earn larger profits than a competitive industry. If the only effect of monopoly were to transfer resources from consumers to the monopolist, the case against monopoly would have to rest entirely on its effects on the distribution of income. Most price theory texts make it clear, though, that besides affecting the distribution of income, monopoly imposes a net loss on society—even when the monopolist is included in society. Only under very implausible conditions can a system of unregulated markets function efficiently if monopoly is present.

The proof of the proposition just stated can be carried out under very weak assumptions. If one wants to obtain a quantitative measure of welfare loss due to monopoly, however, strong assumptions must generally be made. Suppose that for all consumers both the income elasticity of demand for a particular good and the fraction of income spent on that good are small. Then if the ith consumer purchases a quantity q^i at a price P, the area under his demand curve from the $q = 0$ axis to $q = q^i$ can serve as an approximate dollar measure of the addition to his total utility from consuming the good in question. If society values the income of all its members equally, the corresponding area under the demand curve for a consumer-good industry can be used as a measure of community welfare. (This analysis is approximately correct if some sales are made to perfectly competitive consumer-good industries, rather than directly to consumers.)

For the purposes of this exercise, assume that the above assumptions are sensible for this industry. Figure 5.1 then illustrates the computation of the welfare loss due to monopoly. A monopolist will charge a price P_M and sell a quantity Q_M. The total area under the industry demand curve from the $Q = 0$ axis to $Q = Q_M$ is the sum of the areas labeled A, B, C, D, and F. The sum of $C + D + F$, which is just $P_M Q_M$, is paid to the monopolist by consumers, while $A + B$ is the so-called net consumer's surplus. The total cost of producing Q_M is equal to $F + FC$, where FC is the monopolist's fixed costs, if any. Since the cost of production represents use of society's resources, the "net welfare" associated with

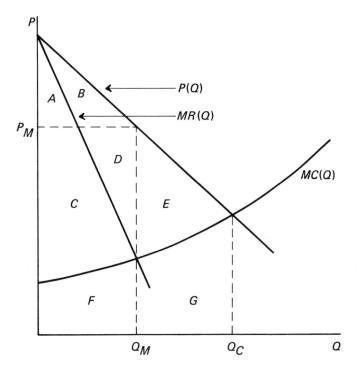

Figure 5.1 Welfare loss due to monopoly.

the monopoly is simply

$$A + B + C + D - FC$$

This area can also be derived directly by adding net consumer's surplus, $A + B$, to monopoly profits, $C + D - FC$.

Suppose now that $MC(Q)$, the monopoly's marginal cost curve, is the supply curve of a competitive industry which could replace it. Then an amount Q_C would be produced if the industry were competitive. The same analysis we just worked through indicates that the net welfare associated with the competitive industry would be

$$A + B + C + D + E - FC$$

Subtracting, the net welfare loss due to monopoly is the area labeled E. Note that this is a *net* loss; we've considered the monopolist on a par with all other members of society. The simplest way to compute E is to notice that it is equal to the area under $P(Q)$ from Q_M to Q_C minus the additional cost incurred in order to produce Q_C.

As an interested citizen you should use the technique just presented to compute the welfare loss due to monopoly in your industry in the short run and in the long run.

Thoughts on Reports

As we mentioned in Chapter 3, a good research report moves from assumptions to method to results. That outline makes sense here as well.

You might begin by presenting the estimated cost and demand functions you will work with. Substitute in the values of the exogenous variables and of N_0 in order to obtain the functions appropriate for this exercise. You can then outline the methods used to obtain the forecasts of short-run and long-run equilibria and present your numerical results. The arithmetic should probably be confined to an appendix. Method is probably more important than results, but incorrect arithmetic here can cause you trouble in the decision-making exercise.

PRICING IN OLIGOPOLISTIC MARKETS

6

Introduction

The simplest definition of the word oligopoly comes from its Greek roots; these translate simply as *few sellers*. Of course, *few* is one of those relative words that should never appear in a good definition, for the question "How few?" immediately arises. Here we mean few enough so that each firm is aware that its profits depend on the decisions of each other firm in the industry. In more general terms, an oligopoly is a group of firms selling similar or identical products, each member of which recognizes the impact of each other member's actions on its profit.

In the usual model of perfectly competitive markets, firms are assumed to be so numerous that the actions of any one can have no perceptible effect on the others. At the opposite extreme, a monopolist has no competitors to worry about. In both these polar cases, there is little competition as a businessman might define the term, since there is no need for conscious consideration of other sellers.

One important distinguishing feature of oligopoly is that there is no general relation between industry and firm demand. An oligopolist knows that it is likely that his rivals will, at least eventually, become aware of any price change he institutes. The eventual change in sales he can expect to result from a change in his price depends on his rivals' reactions to the change. Since these reactions usually cannot be known in advance, each firm's decisions will be based on the response it expects each of its possible actions to elicit from the other firms in the industry. It is the basic importance of *expectations* in concentrated markets that makes it difficult to draw precise conclusions about oligopoly behavior. This chapter outlines in general terms some of what is known and believed about the relations between oligopoly market structure and behavior. Our discussion is based on careful analyses of industry behavior by empirically oriented economists as well as on deductive theory.

The bulk of our discussion in this chapter focuses on price competition. The second section considers the oligopoly problem in the static case where firms set price once and only once. We then bring in dynamic considerations in the third section, examining the more realistic situation where each firm may change its price at any time. In these two sections it is assumed that entry into the industry is impossible; this assumption is relaxed in the fourth section.

The last section of this chapter summarizes the conclusions of the preceding sections and briefly considers nonprice competition, in which such competitive tools as advertising and research are employed. This form of rivalry is quite important in many industries. Our discussion of this aspect of behavior concludes, in general, that many of the things we say about price competition are also true of nonprice competition.

Most of the discussion here assumes, as did all of Chapter 4, that firms seek to maximize profit. As we indicated there, that assumption is most easily defended under competitive conditions. In oligopolistic or monopolistic markets, the lack of competitive pressures may enable business managements to pursue other goals. Theories of firms which do not maximize profits are still in a fairly crude state, however, and most applied economists do not seem to find them very useful. The references at the end of the chapter contain discussions of these theories as well as more conventional analyses of oligopoly.

The Static Problem

The essence of the situation facing oligopolists is captured by the so-called prisoner's dilemma game, which describes the following situation. Two persons are arrested for robbery. Each is given the chance to testify against the other. If neither testifies, both will spend a year in prison on a minor charge. If both testify, both will spend 10 years in prison. If one testifies and the other doesn't, the one that says nothing will be sentenced to 20 years and the informant will go free.

It is clearly in the interest of both prisoners that neither testify. But if they are not allowed to talk with each other, it is very likely that both will testify. By testifying each can ensure that he will spend no more than 10 years in prison, while if either refuses to talk, he may end up in jail for twice as long.

A concentrated market situation bears a striking resemblance to this simple game. If all firms charge high prices, all will generally earn a high profit. If all charge low prices, all will earn little. This might suggest that high prices would always prevail. But the situation is unstable in the same way the prisoner's dilemma game is: if all firms but one charge high prices, and that one firm undercuts the others, the sly one will generally earn a very large profit. Thus all firms have a strong incentive to persuade their rivals to charge high prices; the incentive to follow them is weaker.

We therefore identify two basic tendencies in oligopolies. The first is the tendency for all firms to try to band together to raise prices and to keep them high, to *collude* explicitly or implicitly. A group of firms which have explicitly agreed to coordinate their actions and limit competition for mutual benefit is called a *cartel*. If successful, a collusive agreement can maximize total profits for the group of firms participating. The second tendency results from the fact that any firm can maximize its individual profits by *cheating* on an agreement to charge high prices, so that any collusive agreement may very well be unstable. The basic concern of this chapter is to identify and discuss factors affecting the formation and stability of collusive agreements.

A simple duopoly (two sellers) example will further illuminate the basic features of concentrated markets. Suppose there are two firms, selling amounts Q_1 and Q_2 of identical products. Industry price, P, is determined by the simple demand relation

$$P = A - B(Q_1 + Q_2) \qquad (6\text{-}1)$$

where A and B are positive constants. For simplicity, we assume that total cost is zero for both firms. If we let total industry output be Q, it is clear that industry revenue and profit is given by

$$R = PQ = AQ - BQ^2 \qquad (6\text{-}2)$$

Revenue, and hence total profit, is maximized if $Q = A/2B$. Thus for maximum industry profits, the firms should agree to set $Q_1 = Q_2 = A/4B$. Each firm would then earn a profit of $A^2/8B$.

Now suppose that firm one adheres faithfully to an agreement to sell $A/4B$ units. If firm two knows that firm one will do this, its profit is given by

$$R_2 = PQ_2 = AQ_2 - B[(A/4B) + Q_2]Q_2 \qquad (6\text{-}3)$$

Firm two's profit can easily be shown to be maximized by $Q_2 = 3A/8B$. This yields a market price of $3A/8$, firm two's revenue would be $9A^2/64B$, and firm one would earn $3A^2/32B$, two-thirds of firm two's earnings. Total industry profits would be less than they would have been in the obvious collusive solution, but firm two would be better off. (Total profits may decline further, and firm two's profits may fall below the cartel level, if firm one were to retaliate. We return to this point below.)

Ignoring the possibility of price change and of outsiders entering the industry, let us consider some general factors affecting the formation and stability of collusive agreements. (A situation where these assumptions are not unreasonably restrictive might be a group of firms submitting sealed bids on a unique, large government project.)

The first consideration is the *legal structure* the industry is operating under. If an agreement to charge high prices can be written up as an enforceable contract, the agreement will be more stable than if this is not possible. This guarantee of stability, in turn, gives individual firms a greater incentive to enter the agreement, since the likelihood that they will be cheated is reduced.

Another consideration is whether profit-sharing schemes can be drawn up and enforced. If this possibility exists, for example, firms can decide which one of them will be the low bidder on a project and then agree to share the profits earned by that company.

Under the English common law, agreements to fix prices or to share profits (or markets) are not illegal, but they cannot be enforced in court. The likelihood of stable collusive action is reduced when judicial procedures cannot be used to punish cheaters.

Under the Sherman Antitrust Act, any overt agreement among firms which either directly or indirectly acts to restrict competition is illegal. U.S. firms can legally only attempt to implicitly or tacitly collude on price policies, and no legal sanctions can be brought to bear on cheaters. Thus the American legal structure works against the formation of stable collusive agreements both by limiting the power of an industry to maintain pricing discipline and by restricting communications among industry members. Under the common law, firms could meet to discuss and agree on prices; this is quite illegal under the Sherman Act. As a general rule, anything which makes communication among actual or potential industry members more difficult works against a stable collusive agreement. The greater the *number of firms* in an industry, for instance, the more difficult it will be to organize a collusive agreement.

Another influence is the *similarity of the firms*. If all firms in an industry are identical, and if all have the same perceptions of the present and expectations about the future, it will be easy for them to agree on the strategy which will maximize total industry profit and provide each firm with identical earnings. But if firms' cost structures differ, for instance, a problem arises because the strategy that maximizes total industry profits may leave some firms badly off. For example, it may be optimal for all production to be done by the most efficient company. In such cases, it would be necessary for the firms that stand to gain the most to compensate those that would be harmed by the agreement before the latter could be induced to enter into it. Even if direct cash transfers, or *side payments* as they are often called, are permitted by law (the legal structure enters again), it may be difficult to agree on the amounts to be paid. If side payments are illegal, it becomes even more difficult to obtain and sustain agreement among firms with different cost structures.

Similarly, if firms' views of present and future demand and cost conditions differ drastically, it may be impossible to form a cartel, simply because the potential members cannot agree on its optimal policy. If explicit discussions of joint actions do not or cannot take place, so that reliance must be placed on tacit understandings, stable collusion is even less likely.

Finally, we consider the *incentive for cheating* on a cartel or on an implicit collusive agreement. Both demand and cost conditions are important here. The more responsive demand is to price differences within an industry, the greater the incentive to cheat on any price-fixing agreement. Generally, if the products of a group of sellers are viewed as nearly identical by buyers, each firm will find that the demand for its output is very responsive to the price it charges. Under such conditions, the incentive to cheat on a cartel can be quite enormous. This makes for instability of any agreement, but it may make the formation of an agreement more likely. If the firms each stand to lose a great deal if they are undercut, they may repeatedly try to set up mechanisms that will make undercutting less likely. This is especially true if total industry demand is price-inelastic, so that the difference between cartel and competitive profits is large. On the other hand, to the extent that products are *differentiated* in the minds of buyers, the vulnerability of an agreement to cheating is reduced, but the incentive to collude in the first place may be also lessened. The usual expectation is that, since the incentive to cheat is less when products are differentiated, an industry is more likely to have a stable collusive agreement in this case, and the agreement will very likely be implicit.

The impact of product differentiation on the

incentive to cheat can be illustrated algebraically. Consider a market with two sellers whose products are not viewed as identical by consumers. The firms set prices P_1 and P_2, and sales are determined by the demand relations

$$Q_1 = a + kP_2 - (b + k)P_1 \quad \text{and}$$

$$Q_2 = a + kP_1 - (b + k)P_2 \quad (6\text{-}4)$$

where a, b, and k are positive constants. Industry demand when both firms charge a price P is found by adding these equations, yielding

$$(Q_1 + Q_2) = 2a - 2bP \quad (6\text{-}5)$$

The larger is k, the more sensitive the industry's customers are to price differences within the industry. When k is very large, the two firms are producing the products which the market considers identical. If $k = 0$, both firms are pure monopolists.

Assume, for simplicity, that both firms have zero costs. Then total profits are maximized when $P_1 = P_2 = a/2b$. If both firms charge this price, both earn a profit of $a^2/4b$.

Suppose firm one charges a price of $a/2b$, and firm two feels that his competitor will maintain that price no matter what. Then firm two's profit can be written as

$$R_2 = [a + (ak/2b)]P_2 - (b + k)(P_2)^2 \quad (6\text{-}6)$$

This quantity is maximized by $P_2 = P_2^* = (a/2b)[(2b + k)/(2b + 2k)]$. Notice that for $k = 0$, there is no incentive to cheat. The larger is k, the lower is the optimal cheating price. Substituting the expression for P_2^* into (6-6), we find that the cheater's profit is given by

$$R_2^* = \frac{a^2}{4b}\frac{(2b + k)^2}{4b(b + k)} = \frac{a^2}{4b}\left[1 + \frac{k^2}{4b(b + k)}\right] \quad (6\text{-}7)$$

Equation (6-7) rises when k is increased, as can be verified by differentiating $k^2/(b + k)$ with respect to k. Thus the less differentiated the products, the greater the incentive to cheat.

Cost conditions also affect the incentives to cheat on an implicit or explicit collusive agreement. The more rapidly marginal cost rises, the less the incentive to lower price to acquire additional sales. Similarly, the more short-run excess capacity a firm has, the greater its incentive to cheat.

In this static analysis, we have identified a number of forces that affect the stability of collusive agreements. The most important were the legal structure in the economy, the number of firms in the industry, factors affecting communications among the firms, similarity of firms, and the incentives to cheat on a cartel agreement as determined by demand and cost conditions. We next relax the assumption that firms' prices (and conditions in the industry in general) do not change. Additional forces affecting cartel stability will be suggested, and additional effects of the elements discussed above will be examined.

The Dynamic Problem

We still retain the assumption that no outside firm can enter the industry. Further, we assume that the firms are not parties to an enforceable cartel agreement. The new element in our analysis is the fact that demand and cost conditions and prices may change over time, and firms' strategies must take this into account.

The problem of finding an optimal collusive strategy is now replaced by the problem of first finding such a strategy and then modifying it as circumstances change. Thus anything that makes it difficult to decide on an optimal strategy will make it even more difficult for the industry to respond in a coordinated fashion to changes in its environment, since effecting such responses amounts to renegotiating the collusive policy. Legal structures or numbers of firms that make face-to-face negotiation difficult will lessen the ability of the industry to react cooperatively to change, and an agreement that cannot react to changes in its environment will collapse. The more diverse the products sold by an industry, the more difficult it is to reach and sustain a collusive agreement, since more prices must be decided upon. The classic example of this problem is the cement industry, where transportation costs are so important that it would be quite irrational for price not to depend on the buyer's location. Conceivably, there could be as many prices as buyers. The basing-point system was employed by the cement industry (and the steel industry) to simplify the price structure artificially and thus to make the implicit collusive agreement simpler.

It may be easier to structure and operate a collusive agreement, especially a tacit one, if the industry has a *dominant firm*. Then the dominant firm is the obvious leader, and it is easy for the other firms to agree to follow its lead. The dominant firm's actions are then unambiguous signals to the other producers. It may be difficult to sustain stability, though, since it may be hard for the dominant firm to detect cheating. Also, any effort on its part to punish cheaters may weaken the collusive agreement.

The major change in the model when we bring in dynamic elements is the nature of cheating on an explicit or implicit agreement. Given the ability of the faithful parties to the agreement to alter their prices, it becomes likely that a cheater will eventually face retaliation. Besides considering the short-run sales and profits gained by breaking the agreement, a potential cheater must consider the impact of retaliation. If his action depresses everyone's profits, including his, for a long time to come, this may outweigh his short-run gains.

An important aspect of retaliation is the time until it occurs, the *reaction lag*. This can be divided into two intervals: the time it takes to detect cheating and the time it takes to effect a response. The longer cheating can go undetected, the more profit the cheater will make. Similarly, the longer it takes the faithful firms to respond to a cheater once they're aware of him, the more profitable it is to cheat.

The other dimension which must be considered by a potential cheater is the form of the other firms' response to his action. If the others do nothing, he will continue to earn very high profits. If the others merely match his low price, and if there is some reaction lag, cheating will still usually be profitable. If the others react by undercutting the cheater, however, cheating can be rendered unprofitable.

It will clarify things somewhat if we now formally examine the dynamic problem facing a potential cheater. Let r be the rate of interest used to discount future earnings, and assume that interest is compounded continuously. Then it is easy to show that one dollar invested today will build into e^{rt} dollars in t periods, where e is the base of the system of Naperian or natural logarithms. One dollar to be paid t periods in the future (t need not be an integer) is worth e^{-rt} dollars today. We write this quantity as $\exp(-rt)$. When either r or t is zero, this quantity equals one, and it declines to zero as rt becomes large.

Suppose that the potential cheater could earn profits of R^L per period if he remained loyal to the agreement. If he cheats, he expects to earn profits of R^C until his cheating is detected. He expects to be detected after τ periods. At this point his wronged competitors will retaliate, and then he expects to earn R^W for T periods. At the end of $T + \tau$ periods, the industry is expected to reestablish the initial equilibrium, and he will earn R^L once again. We assume that R^C is greater than R^L, which in turn is greater than R^W.

We first consider the case where r is zero. Then the total profit from remaining loyal is just $R^L(T + \tau)$, while a cheater will earn $R^C \tau + R^W T$. The ratio of total profits from cheating to total profits from remaining loyal can be written as

$$T^C/T^L = (R^C/F^L)F^0 + (R^W/R^L)(1 - F^0) \qquad (6\text{-}8)$$

where $\qquad F^0 = \tau/(T + \tau)$

The incentive to cheat clearly rises with R^C and R^W and falls with R^L. Similarly, it is never profitable to cheat if τ is zero or if T is very large.

Now suppose that r is nonzero, so that one dollar today is indeed worth more than one dollar to be paid tomorrow. Recall from integral calculus that

$$\int_{T_1}^{T_2} k \, \exp(-rt) \, dt = (k/r)$$

$$[\exp(-rT_1) - \exp(-rT_2)] \quad (6\text{-}9)$$

for any constant k. The *present discounted value* of the profits of a loyal firm is given by

$$PV^L = \int^{T+\tau} R^L \, \exp(-rt) \, dt$$

$$= (R^L/r)(1 - \exp[-r(T + \tau)]) \qquad (6\text{-}10)$$

employing (6-9). Similarly, the present value of a cheater's profits is

$$PV^C = (R^C/r)[1 - \exp(-r\tau)] + (R^W/r)$$

$$(\exp(-r\tau) - \exp[-r(T + \tau)]) \quad (6\text{-}11)$$

Cheating will be profitable if and only if PV^C is

greater than PV^L. The ratio of these two quantities may be written as

$$PV^C/PV^L = (R^C/R^L)F^r + (R^W/R^L)(1 - F^r)$$

where   (6-12)

$$F^r = [1 - \exp(-r\tau)]/(1 - \exp[-r(T + \tau)])$$

Thus (6-12) is a weighted average of the same sort as (6-8); it is easy to show that as r goes to zero, F^r approaches F^0.

The larger is F^r the more likely it is that cheating is profitable. When $\tau = 0$, when detection is instant, F^r is zero, and cheating is never profitable. When r is very large, a dollar earned today is worth much more than a dollar lost tomorrow, and cheating is likely to become profitable. When T is zero, cheating is also always profitable. When T is very large, F^r reduces to $[1 - \exp(-r\tau)]$. For any r, it will then always be possible to find a τ small enough to make F^r so small that cheating is unprofitable.

Notice that all the quantities in (6-8) and (6-12), except for r and R^L, are values *expected* by the potential cheater. The problem of an industry wishing to deter price cutting is thus to influence the *expectations* of its members about the values of the parameters that determine the profitability of breaking whatever agreement sustains high prices. If all firms feel that cheating would not be profitable, none will cheat, even though all may be wrong.

We must now consider the *information* available to each firm that can be used to detect cheating. If each knows the others' prices, detection of cheating is trivial. A trade association that is legally empowered to obtain and publish prices, for instance, makes for stability of collusion. A voluntary association is, of course, vulnerable to false price reports by cheating firms.

If each firm can detect cheating only by analyzing changes in its own sales, the detection problem is more difficult. Each firm must then make a judgment about which sales changes are attributable to fluctuations in the myriad variables determining demand and which are due to a rival's cheating. If the number of firms is large, individual firms will usually be unable to do this with any confidence. Under perfect competition each firm is so small that it is unable to noticeably influence any individual competitor. Similarly, no firm can, by itself, detect any alteration in the policies of any other single company. No collusive agreement can be stable under these conditions, as many farmers' organizations have found to their sorrow.

All other things equal, it is clear that the more predictable individual firms' demands are, the easier it is to detect cheating. The more "noise" there is in the market, the harder it will be to detect a price-cutter.

The problem faced by a potential cheater in a dynamic setting is thus quite complicated. The cheater must estimate his short-run gains, as before; cost and demand conditions still affect the profitability of cheating. But a potential cheater must also consider how long it would take the other firms to detect his action, and he must take into account his expectations concerning the form of their reaction to his cheating. Both these, especially the first, are inherently uncertain. The cheater's optimal strategy thus depends on his *estimates of the probabilities* involved and, quite fundamentally, on his *attitude toward risk*. Even if profits promise on average to be lower for a faithful firm than for a cheater, a firm may elect to remain faithful simply because that is the less risky course. Firms which are not solely concerned with profit are especially likely to avoid the risks and ill feelings chiseling brings.

Once cheating is detected, subsequent behavior can be quite interesting. We shall present two special scenarios which have the advantage of illustrating the sort of noncollusive or *noncooperative equilibria* often encountered in theoretical discussions of oligopoly.

Consider first the duopoly (oligopoly with two firms) selling identical products with demand structure given by Eq. (6-1). Below that equation we discussed the case where firm two cheated on a collusive agreement, assuming that firm one would not respond. Suppose now that firm one does in fact respond. It can set any output at all, but a sensible move would be to maximize its profits given firm two's output, $Q_2 = 3A/8B$. If it does this, it will produce and sell $5A/16B$, undercutting firm two by maximizing $R_1 = PQ_1 = AQ_1 - B[(3A/8B) + Q_1] Q_1$.

If firm two retaliates in the same fashion and the process continues, equilibrium will be reached at the point where both firms are producing $A/3B$. This point is called the *Cournot equilibrium point*. It is stable in the sense that neither firm has an incentive to make a unilateral change in output. But, of course, both would be better off if they could reestablish $Q_1 = Q_2 = A/4B$. It should be noted that the Cournot equilibrium point can easily be computed when there are N firms in the market; total output rises with N.

We can quickly show that the point $Q_1 = Q_2 = A/3B$ is indeed a noncooperative equilibrium in this model. Consider the problem of maximizing the profit of firm one, assuming that the output of firm two will not change. To solve this, we must maximize

$$AQ_1 - B(Q_1 + Q_2)Q_1 \qquad (6\text{-}13)$$

treating Q_2 as a constant. Differentiating (6-13) with respect to Q_1 and setting the derivative equal to zero, we obtain

$$A - BQ_2 - 2BQ_1 = 0 \qquad (6\text{-}14)$$

Equation (6-14) gives Q_1 as a function of Q_2.

If we similarly consider maximizing the profit of firm two under the assumption that Q_1 is a constant, we find that optimal Q_2 is determined as a function of Q_1 according to

$$A - BQ_1 - 2BQ_2 = 0 \qquad (6\text{-}15)$$

If both (6-14) and (6-15) are satisfied, neither firm has any incentive to unilaterally alter its production, and the corresponding Q_1, Q_2 pair is a noncooperative equilibrium point. Solving (6-14) and (6-15) yields $Q_1 = Q_2 = A/3B$.

Now let us consider a duopoly with differentiated products, as described by demand schedules (6-4). Total industry profits are maximized when $P_1 = P_2 = a/2b$, as we argued above. If firm one is faithful to an agreement to charge this price, firm two can maximize its profits by setting $P_2 = (a/2b)[(2b + k)/(2b + 2k)]$, as we saw above. When it detects cheating, firm one might sensibly retaliate by maximizing its profits given the price charged by firm two, thus setting a price below firm two's. If firm two then responds in the same fashion, the process will continue until prices have fallen to the point where $P_1 = P_2 = a/(2b + k)$, the *Edgeworth-Bertrand equilibrium point*. At this point, neither firm has an incentive to unilaterally lower price further, though both would probably seek to restore a price of $a/2b$. Notice that when k is very large, price cutting does not stop until price is zero (or until price is equal to marginal cost, when marginal cost is positive).

To prove that $P_1 = P_2 = a/(2b + k)$ is really a noncollusive equilibrium, we proceed as before. Consider the problem of maximizing the profits of firm one, given the price of firm two. Firm one will then maximize

$$aP_1 + kP_1P_2 - (b + k)(P_1)^2 \qquad (6\text{-}16)$$

with respect to P_1, treating P_2 as a constant. Setting the first derivative of (6-16) equal to zero, we obtain

$$a + kP_2 - 2(b + k)P_1 = 0 \qquad (6\text{-}17)$$

This equation gives P_1 as a function of P_2.

To obtain P_2 as a function of P_1, we maximize the profit of the second firm, treating P_1 as a constant; this yields

$$a + kP_1 - 2(b + k)P_2 = 0 \qquad (6\text{-}18)$$

In order for neither firm to have an incentive for a unilateral price change, both (6-16) and (6-17) must be satisfied. It is easily seen that they will be satisfied if and only if $P_1 = P_2 = a/(2b + k)$.

Neither of these duopoly models allows for positive, nonconstant marginal cost. The reader might examine how the results are modified when positive costs are introduced. It is also possible to solve these models with more general demand functions, stating results in terms of elasticities. Finally, the interested reader might find it profitable to explore the implications of capacity constraints in these models.

In the presence of imperfect information and risk, the simple faithful firm-cheater dichotomy may be a bit unrealistic. A firm may lower its price as a signal to other firms about where it thinks the optimal price should be. The others must, somehow, distinguish this from cheating. As we saw above, the incentive to cheat generally rises as profits rise, and an industry may find it best not to attempt to maximize total industry profits. It may instead maintain price at a level below the profit-maximizing level in order to reduce the incentive to cheat and thus to increase stability. The level at which price stabilizes will then depend on the mutual trust of the various firms, as well as on their attitudes toward and estimates of risk. A cheater may, by his action, lower the level of trust to a point where it is impossible for the industry ever to attain maximum total profits.

The above analysis has considered oligopoly behavior as a dynamic problem in the face of risk. Attitudes toward risk were seen to affect firms' strategies. We saw that the rate at which future profits are discounted will also influence industry behavior, since a cheater must weigh gains today against probable losses in the future. Other new elements were the information available to firms, especially as regards their ability to detect cheating, the ability of the industry to respond to cheating and the form of that response, and the level of trust in the industry. So far, we have taken the number of firms in the industry as given, and we next relax this assumption.

The Impact of Potential Entry

In the perfectly competitive model, firms are assumed able to enter and leave industries instantly and costlessly. It is further assumed that firms will enter industries where excess profits are being earned and leave industries where profits fail to cover opportunity cost. The textbook monopoly model begins by assuming that no firms can enter the monopolist's industry, no matter what he does. As one might expect, conditions of entry in the real world are usually somewhere between these extremes. There are *barriers to entry*, but these are not usually so great as to completely exclude new firms from entering any particular industry.

The literature distinguishes three basic kinds of barriers. The first is *absolute cost* differences between new and established firms. Established firms may have critical patents or important know-how, or they may control the most desirable raw-material sources. It is often alleged that the capital market favors established firms, so that new entrants must pay a higher price for investment funds.

A second problem confronting potential entrants has to do with *relative size*. The larger the minimum efficient firm size necessary to capture economies of scale relative to total sales in a particular market, the less easily an entrant can sneak unnoticed into that market, and the more likely his entry is to upset prevailing patterns of price formation. If, for instance, a firm need only produce 1% of the current total output of a particular industry in order to have the same average cost as the established firms, he can probably enter the industry safely assuming that he will not be noticed. His entry is unlikely to cause a sizeable fall in price. On the other hand, if a firm would need to produce 50% of current industry sales in order to be efficient, his entry would add 50% to industry output. Prices would fall, behavior patterns would likely change, and the final equilibrium of the industry would be uncertain.

Finally, the literature often speaks of *product-differentiation* barriers to entry. The stronger are the preferences of buyers for the products of existing firms, the more an entrant is at a disadvantage. If he can change these tastes only with a protracted, massive advertising campaign, the necessity of carrying out such a campaign can sometimes constitute a barrier to entry.

The best way to consider entry is as a random process, with the probability of entry in any time period varying inversely with the level of barriers to entry and directly with the profits being earned by the established firms. The likelihood of entry will also depend heavily on how potential entrants expect the established firms to react to entry; the problem of deterring entry is very much like the problem of preventing cheating. If potential entrants feel the existing firms would not change their price and output policies if entry occurred, entry is more likely.

On the other hand, if the established firms can convince potential entrants that their entry would send prices tumbling, entry is less likely. Given entry barriers and the expectations of potential entrants, there will generally be some level of excess profits, greater than zero, that can be earned by the established firms that will make the probability of entry zero, though the optimal collusive strategy may well be to earn higher profits and tolerate a positive probability of entry.

How does the possibility of entry affect oligopoly behavior? It seems likely that the impact on the stability of collusive agreements will generally not be great. Conditions of entry must be considered by the parties to any such agreement, of course, and to the extent that these firms disagree about how to handle the threat of entry, the agreement is less stable. But it is not likely that the height of entry barriers will have much direct effect on the agreement's stability.

The main impact of barriers to entry would seem to be on optimal industry strategy. If an industry seeks to maximize total profits, it must consider the possibility that a strategy that maximizes profits in the short run will induce entry and thereby result in lower profits in the long run. As before, short-run gains must be weighed against the possibility of long-run losses. In general, the lower are entry barriers, the lower will be the industry's optimum price.

Summary and Conclusions

So far we have explicitly considered only price (or output competition. It should be intuitively clear that the same basic conceptual framework applies to other forms of competition as well. Consider, for instance, advertising. It is generally the case in established industries that if all firms can agree to agree on the levels of advertising budgets, they can coordinate their spending so as to maximize industry profits. If all increase advertising budgets above their optimal levels, all will make less money. But if all firms but one are adhering to the agreed-upon advertising policy, and one firm is advertising more than its quota, the cheater stands to gain. We have the prisoner's dilemma again, and the rest of our discussion above can be applied more or less directly to nonprice competition.

The main difference between price and nonprice competition is that agreements to limit nonprice competition are generally quite difficult to formulate and enforce. There are so many forms of nonprice competition that if one, say, the number of salesmen, is controlled, firms can easily cheat on the spirit of the agreement by using another form, say, advertising, more intensively. In addition, it is more difficult to detect cheating on the letter of an agreement on nonprice competition. The impact of advertising on sales is not generally easy to predict, and firms do not normally publish their advertising budgets. It would thus be very difficult to detect violations of an agreement to limit advertising spending. In some cases these problems can be circumvented by agreements directly assigning individual buyers to individual sellers, but this is not usually possible. (It is illegal in this country.) As a consequence, successful collusion to limit nonprice competition is quite rare.

We can summarize the analysis of this chapter by grouping the factors we have considered under three broad headings. First are those that affect the ability of firms in an industry to agree on the policy that will maximize their total profits, the optimal collusive strategy. Second are those forces that affect the ability of colluding firms to obtain high profits. Finally, there are those factors that directly influence the stability of collusive agreements.

The greater the degree of communication among the firms in an industry, the greater the likelihood that they can agree on a joint strategy. Communication possibilities will be affected by, among other things, the legal structure and the number of firms involved. The more nearly identical firms' cost structures and views of their environment, the easier it will be to arrive at an agreement. Finally, the simpler a good agreement can be, the more likely one is to be formulated. If all firms sell one product at one price, agreement will be easier than if each sells a variety of products in a variety of locations at a variety of prices.

The lower are entry barriers and the more strongly potential entrants expect the industry to react to their entry, the greater are potential industry profits. The less likely high profits are to attract antitrust prosecution, the more likely it is that an industry will be able to maximize its profits. The more the members of an industry trust each other, the more likely it is that they will be willing to charge the price that maximizes their total profits, even though this price may render cheating very profitable. Two other general considerations interact with all these elements. The more tolerant the members of the industry are to risk, the more likely it is that they will seek the highest possible profits. Finally, the more heavily future profits are discounted (that is, the higher the relevant interest rate), the more likely it is that colluding firms will pursue a strategy that maximizes current profits.

The stability of collusive agreements is affected by a wide variety of forces. The more sensitive demand is to price differentials within an industry, the flatter are marginal cost curves; the greater is excess capacity, the greater will be the immediate profits earned by a cheater. The more effectively each firm expects his rivals to respond to any cheating, and the quicker they can do so, the less the incentive to cheat. The speed of industry response will be positively related to the amount of information available to each firm that helps to detect cheating. All other things equal, it will be easier to detect cheating the fewer the firms in the industry and the more stable each firm's demand. Since cheating is usually risky, the less tolerant firms are of risk, the less likely they are to cheat. The more heavily they discount future profits as opposed to present profits, the more likely they are to cheat. Finally, the less tolerant the legal system is of formal cartel arrangements, the more likely is cheating.

It should be obvious that a large number of forces influence conduct in oligopolistic industries. The net impact of any one on industry profits may be difficult to ascertain. We do have some insights about how concentrated industries perform, although these observations by no means constitute a fully developed theory.

REFERENCES

A large number of authors have considered the motivations of business managements and how their goals might translate into observable behavior. Four important discussions of these efforts are

Baumol, W. J., *Business Behavior, Value and Growth*, The Macmillan Company, New York, 1959.

Cyert, R. M., and J. G. March, *A Behavioral Theory of the Firm*, Prentice-Hall, Inc., Englewood Cliffs, New Jersey, 1963.

Machlup, F., "Theories of the Firm: Marginalist, Behavioral, Managerial," *American Economic Review,* 57 (March, 1967), 1—33.

Williamson, O. E., *The Economics of Discretionary Behavior: Managerial Objectives in a Theory of the Firm,* Prentice-Hall, Inc., Englewood Cliffs, New Jersey, 1964.

Machlup's paper comments on the new approaches, while the other three references present non-profit-maximizing theories of the firm in some detail.

Many price theory texts do not discuss oligopoly theory in much depth. Two notable exceptions are

Stigler, G. J., *The Theory of Price*, Third Edition, The Macmillan Company, New York, 1966, Chapters 12 and 13.

Watson, D. S., *Price Theory and its Uses*, Second Edition, Houghton Mifflin Company, Boston, 1968, Chapters 19 and 20.

Since Cournot presented his model in 1838, an awful lot has been written about oligopoly behavior without producing anything like a definitive theory. A sampling from the following list should convey some of the flavor of the investigations.

Bishop, R. L., "Duopoly: Collusion or Warfare," *American Economic Review*, 59 (September, 1960), 933–961.

Fellner, W., *Competition Among the Few*, Alfred A. Knopf, Inc., New York, 1949.

Heflebower, R. B., and G. W. Stocking, eds. (for the American Economic Association), *Readings in Industrial Organization and Public Policy*, Richard D. Irwin, Inc., Homewood, Illinois, 1958, especially Readings 4–7, 9, 10, 12, and 17.

Orr, D., and P. W. MacAvoy, "Price Strategies to Promote Cartel Stability," *Economica*, 32 (May, 1965), 186–197.

Scherer, F. M., *Industrial Market Structure and Economic Performance*, Rand McNally & Co., Chicago, 1970, especially Chapters 5–9.

Stigler, G. J., *The Organization of Industry*, Richard D. Irwin, Inc., Homewood, Illinois, 1968, especially Chapters 5, 6, 16, and 18.

Stigler, G. J., and K. E. Boulding, eds. (for the American Economic Association), *Readings in Price Theory*, Richard D. Irwin, Inc., Homewood, Illinois, 1952, Readings 18–22.

The impact of conditions of entry into various industries on firm behavior is discussed in the following two references. Bain's book is a pioneering attempt to measure the importance of various kinds of barriers as well as an interesting investigation of their impact. The chapter by Needham surveys the theoretical literature.

Bain, J. S., *Barriers to New Competition*, Harvard University Press, Cambridge, 1956, especially Chapters 1—5.

Needham, D., *Economic Analysis and Industrial Structure*, Holt, Rinehart & Winston, New York, 1969, Chapter 7.

THE DECISION-MAKING EXERCISE

7

This chapter outlines an exercise primarily designed to illustrate the problems and results of decision-making in oligopolistic markets. The computer program employed is not limited to such cases, though; competition and monopoly can also be simulated.

Students will be divided into teams which are to function as firms. Each firm will begin in a particular industry composed of a number of identical competitors. The sales and profits of each firm will be affected by the prices charged by each one of its competitors. (In the event that more than one industry is simulated, prices in any one industry will have absolutely no effect on the other industries.) The objective during the exercise will be to maximize profits. After the last computer run you will be asked to report on the results of the exercise. The next section outlines the structure of the simulated markets. The third section discusses the mechanics of the exercise, and the chapter concludes with a few suggestions about your report.

Market Structure

Every firm has control over one plant of the type whose cost function you have already estimated. The values of the exogenous variables are the same here as in Chapter 5, so the cost curve $C(q)$ used for the forecasting exercise there is the same one that describes each firm here. Remember that there is an upper limit of 100,000 units on output per period.

Since the values of all exogenous variables are the same as in the forecasting exercise, the plant demand curve $q^d(P)$ obtained there carries over also. This will exercise if all firms charge the same price. (The instructor may raise of lower this curve by multiplying quantity demanded by a constant; you will be told if this has been done.)

When firms charge different prices, industry demand will depend on the unweighted average of the prices of the firms present, while firms' demands will depend on the differences between their price and the industry average. The estimation exercise provides no information on the sensitivity of firm demand to price differences within industries; you will have to learn about this as the exercise progresses. This sensitivity may vary from industry to industry.

You may want to use the observations on cost and demand that are generated during the exercise to sharpen your estimates of the cost function and of the industry demand function. (Both cost and demand functions still contain random disturbance terms.)

Firms are assigned four-digit numbers for identification purposes. The first two digits of this number always refer to the industry in which the firm began operations. For instance, firm three in industry four would be assigned the number 0403, while firm four in the same industry would be designated 0404.

We now must describe the mechanism by which individual firms' decisions are translated into the sales, costs, and profits of all firms in an industry. In particular, it is important to understand the relation between sales and demand. We then discuss four environmental factors that may vary from industry to industry: entry conditions, legality of side payments, legality of collusion, and information availability.

The demand for the output of each firm depends on all prices posted in the market in which the firm operates and on only those prices. If any firm's price is too high, it will receive a zero demand, and it will sell nothing.

Firms for which demand is greater than 100,000 units sell 100,000 units and have unfilled orders equal to the difference between their demand and 100,000. These firms are then put to the side and the computer program divides their unfilled orders among those firms with excess capacity and positive demand. (That is, among those firms with demand greater than zero and less than 100,000.) To do this, it first calculates the total demand in the industry. It then computes the share each of the firms with positive sales and excess capacity received of this total demand. Each then receives a fraction of total unfilled orders equal to its share of total industry demand. Thus if any firm's demand is zero, it will receive no unfilled orders. If the firms with excess capacity accounted for only half of industry demand, they will receive only half of the unfilled orders generated by the other firms. If this allocation raises some demands above 100,000 units, the new unfilled orders so produced are allocated in this same fashion.

The basic idea underlying this mechanism is that a dissatisfied customer does not immediately withdraw his orders. He places some additional orders with firms having excess capacity (and charging higher prices), but his demand is reduced. The process continues until all orders are met or until all firms have unfilled orders. If no unfilled orders are generated, total industry sales will obviously equal total industry demand. If any firms have unfilled orders, though, total industry sales will be less than total industry demand.

A numerical example of this allocation mechanism is shown as Table 7.1. In the first round, demands are simply compared to capacity. Firm four, clearly the firm with the lowest price in the industry, has 90,000 units of unfilled orders, while firms one, two, and three have excess capacity.

In the second round, the unfilled orders are allocated to these three firms in proportion to their shares of original demand. Note that only 42% of firm four's unfilled orders result in additional demand for the outputs of the other firms. At the end of the second round, firm two has new unfilled orders of 14,700 units. In the third round, these orders are allocated between firms one and three, which still have excess capacity. Since firms one and three have the highest prices in the industry, 85% of firm two's unfilled orders are lost to the industry. As the third round generates no new unfilled orders, it is the final round—and the only one which shows on computer output.

Notice that total industry demand was 330,000 units, but, since most of it was concentrated in the hands of firm four, which was unable to satisfy it, total industry sales came to only 266,100 units. Total sales plus unfilled orders equaled 370,400 units—a figure with no meaning at all.

The relation of sales to demand thus depends on what happens to unfilled orders. When there are no

Table 7.1   An Example of the Allocation of Unfilled Orders[a]

Firm	Original demand	Share of original demand
One	10	.03
Two	90	.27
Three	40	.12
Four	190	.58

Round 1			*Round 2*	
Sales	Unfilled orders		Sales	Unfilled orders
10	0	$[10 + (.03)(90) = 12.7]$	12.7	0
90	0	$[90 + (.27)(90) = 114.3]$	100.0	14.3
40	0	$[40 + (.12)(90) = 50.8]$	50.8	0
100	90		100.0	90.0

Round 3		
	Sales	Unfilled orders
$[12.7 + (.03)(14.3) = 13.4]$	13.4	0
	100.0	14.3
$[50.8 + (.12)(14.3) = 52.7]$	52.7	0
	100.0	90.0

[a] All figures are in thousands of units.

unfilled orders in the industry, firms' sales equal their original demands. When unfilled orders are present, it is sometimes possible to compute what firms' demands must have been in order to give rise to the observed distribution of sales and unfilled orders.

At the discretion of the instructor, *it may be possible for outside firms to enter some industries.* The entrant gives up his old plant and begins operating a plant identical to those in the industry he enters. He is, of course, subject to the demand relations that characterize his new industry. A payment, corresponding to the cost of surmounting entry barriers, is assessed each time a firm switches industries; the amount depends on the industry entered. These entry costs will be announced by the instructor. Any attempt to enter an industry into which entry is not allowed will result in the firm being restored to the industry in which it last operated. Any attempt to enter an industry with 10 firms already present will be similarly frustrated, as the computer program supplied is unable to handle industries with more than 10 firms.

Industry demand does not depend on the number of firms present, but firm demand does. If all firms in the industry charge the same price before and after entry or exit, total demand will be unchanged on average. (Remember the disturbance terms.) The effect of entry is to divide the market among all firms present; if there is net exit industry demand is divided among all firms remaining behind. The standard deviation of the disturbance term in firm demand functions rises and falls inversely with the number of firms present; a smaller piece of the action means less absolute variation.

Suppose, for instance, that in period one an industry had four firms each charging two dollars and that in period two another firm entered at the same price. Industry sales would (on average) be the same in the two periods, but each firm in the second period would sell (on average) only four-fifths as much as it did in the first period.

Firms operating in some industries may be permitted to make and receive lump-sum cash transfers (side payments). Payments made to a firm ineligible to receive them or to a nonexistent firm will be debited to the payer but not credited to the payee. Payments made by a firm ineligible to make them will also be debited. Negative side payments will be treated as positive.

The enforceability of contracts calling for side

payments will depend on the legal structure, which is discussed in detail below. Contracts that call only for cash payments will, in general, be enforceable. But contracts that specify a cash payment in exchange for some service that can be held in restraint of trade—such as not entering a particular industry or charging a particular price—will be enforceable only when any and all contracts are enforceable. All enforcements will be handled by the instructor; he will specify the mechanics involved.

There is a *dummy firm* present whose number is 9999. This firm acts as the instructor's fiscal agent. It receives all entry cost payments, and it can make side payments and levy fines. In addition, it can receive payments from any firm.

The extent to which explicit collusion is allowable in price determination will be specified, and it may vary from industry to industry. *Firms will be subject to one of three legal structures:*

1. The Sherman Act. All contracts and conspiracies in restraint of trade are illegal. (You cannot get together to fix price, regulate entry, etc.)
2. The English Common Law. Firms may collude on price and/or agree to make side payments, but such agreements are not enforceable. (The instructor will not fine cheaters for you.)
3. The (Representative) German Kartell Law. Firms may collude on price and/or agree to make side payments, and any such agreements are enforceable.

Again, unless it is stated otherwise, the instructor will perform any and all judicial functions that may be required during this exercise, including interpreting the Sherman Act.

The amount of information given firms operating in each industry about conditions in other industries and about the actions of their competitors may vary from industry to industry at the discretion of the instructor. At a minimum, all firms are shown their own price, sales, profits, and unfilled orders. There are 16 different possible information configurations relating to each industry, including the one in which the firm is currently operating. That is, any, all, or none of the following bits of information may be supplied at the discretion of the instructor: the number of firms present, unweighted average industry price, total industry sales, and total industry profits.

There are 40 different possible configurations of information on each firm's competitors. Any, all, or none of the following bits of information may be supplied a firm about its competitors: the identities of all firms present in its current industry, the identities of entrants only, firms' prices, firms' profits, firms' sales, and firms' unfilled orders. Firms will appear in random order on output lists; it is fruitless to try to infer the actions of a particular firm from its number and the position of data on output lists. Information not available to a particular firm will generally show as a blank on its output sheet in each period.

Mechanics of the Exercise

Each firm must submit a firm card, punched *exactly* as shown in Table 7.2, which will remain in force until a new card is submitted. Be very careful to punch data in the correct columns; there may be penalties for errors. The procedure for submitting firm cards will be announced by the instructor.

At the end of each period's computer run, each firm will receive interim output giving the results of that period's operations. Firms may then elect either to change their firm card or to leave it in force. The time schedule for computer runs will be announced at the start of the exercise.

Making good decisions is not nearly as simple as

Table 7.2 The Format for Firm Cards

Columns	Contents
01–04	The four-digit (no decimal point) firm number—to be assigned. Consists of a two-digit original industry number and a two-digit firm number.
05	Punch an X.
06–07	The industry the firm is to operate in this period. May be left blank if no change in industry is desired.
08	Punch an X.
09–14	The price to be charged. (Punch a decimal point.)
15	Punch an X.
16–19	The four-digit firm number of the firm to which a side payment is to be made. May be left blank if no side payment is to be made.
20	Punch an X.
21–30	The amount of the side payment in dollars. (Punch a decimal point.) This may also be left blank. (If this number is negative it will be made positive by the program.)

the mechanics of presenting them. You would like all firms in your industry to charge the short-run monopoly price, which is the same here as it was in the forecasting problem, unless the instructor has multiplied firm demands by a constant which he has given you. (In this latter case, the new monopoly price is obviously not hard to compute.)

Persuading other firms to charge and stick to the monopoly price will, in general, not be easy. Profits may often be raised dramatically in the short run by undercutting competitors. Against these gains a potential cheater—which means any firm—must weigh the losses that will be imposed by retaliation. In general, you should read and understand Chapter 6 before beginning to make decisions.

The first period of play is particularly difficult in the absence of any explicit cartel agreements. You will almost surely want to set a price somewhere between the short-run competitive and monopoly solutions. Where in this range you select depends, as all your actions in this exercise must, on what you expect your competitors to do.

Thoughts on Reports

At the end of the simulation exercise you will receive a set of summary output giving information on other firms and industries not provided by interim output. In your report you should analyze these data and explain what happened in the exercise. It will generally be useful to employ the concepts developed in the last chapter and to relate industries' performances to their structures. You might formulate and (casually) test some hypotheses.

Particular attention should probably be paid to the firm and industry or industries in which you were involved, since you have information on them not covered in the computer results. But a simple chronology of the actions of a particular firm is of little or no interest here. You should treat this as an exercise in interpreting industrial history, not in writing annual reports.